THE ROAD TO YESTERDAY

THE ROAD TO YESTERDAY

A Memoir

MARYELLEN DONOVAN

as told to Gina Frangello
and Emily Rapp Black

SHE WRITES PRESS

Copyright © 2025 Maryellen Donovan

All rights reserved. No part of this publication may be reproduced, stored in a retrieval system, or transmitted in any form or by any means, electronic, mechanical, photocopying, recording, or otherwise, except for brief quotations in reviews, educational works, or other uses permitted by copyright law.

Published in 2025 by
She Writes Press, an imprint of The Stable Book Group

32 Court Street, Suite 2109
Brooklyn, NY 11201
https://shewritespress.com

Library of Congress Control Number: 2025909819

ISBN: 978-1-64742-956-0
eISBN: 978-1-64742-957-7

Interior Designer: Andrea Reider

Printed in the United States

No part of this publication may be used to train generative artificial intelligence (AI) models. The publisher and author reserve all rights related to the use of this content in machine learning.

All company and product names mentioned in this book may be trademarks or registered trademarks of their respective owners. They are used for identification purposes only and do not imply endorsement or affiliation.

Though you're miles from me now
You're forever on my mind
Some feelings never change
Or fade away with time
The love that you gave to me
Is still living in the heart of me

The Road to Yesterday is a long and winding path
When you think you can't go on
It can always lead you back
To the one you love
The one who makes you smile
You can feel the sunshine in your life for a while
It's just a memory away

Someday I'll hold you close
Like I did back then
Until that moment comes
I'll just remember when
I was wrapped in your arms
It made me feel so safe and warm.

"The Road to Yesterday,"
original song and lyrics by Steve Cherry

TABLE OF CONTENTS

Prologue: Once Upon a Time	ix
Chapter 1: Casserole Days	1
Chapter 2: And It Begins	19
Chapter 3: Expect the Unexpected	29
Chapter 4: My Year of Living Dangerously	53
Chapter 5: Spring Training	74
Chapter 6: The Marriage Plot	93
Chapter 7: Dream a Little Dream	110
Chapter 8: Lightning Strikes Thrice	136
Chapter 9: The Dog Days Are (Almost) Over	164
Epilogue: Because You Believed in Me	189

PROLOGUE: Once Upon a Time

Everything seemed crystalline, sharp, more beautiful than usual. Even the air felt new, with that crisp fall texture that made me imagine leaves crunching under our feet as we moved into fall. The day—and the world—felt fresh. I had just dropped my six-year-old son, Brett, off for his second day of first grade, watched him rush into the earnest swarm of kids all wearing big backpacks across their narrow backs like children pretending to be adults on their way to work. Colton, my baby—cheeks flushed, a wisp of pale hair covering one of his closed eyes—dozed in the car seat as I steered away from the manicured lawns of Greenwich Catholic School and back toward our Stamford, Connecticut, home.

The day was clear and sparkling and perfect—unusually so for September. As the car engine hummed beneath us, I smiled to myself, remembering the night before. I was thirty-seven years old and mother to two boys, and yet I felt giddy as a teenager recalling a first date.

My husband, Steve, and I had been married just two months shy of a decade. Ours was a happy marriage. There were the expected logistical headaches associated with the ongoing renovations to our new dream house in Bedford, New York, as well as the complexities of parenting two small children while also navigating the sometimes-rocky waters of Steve's weekend custody of his sons from his first marriage, but at the end of each day, no matter how challenging conversations or situations became, I always felt secure that this was the man for me, the love of my life. And for the past few months, things between us had been exceptionally romantic and wonderfully charged.

It had been a magical summer. Steve had surprised our family with a last-minute trip to Nantucket, somehow securing an eleventh-hour rental of a gray saltbox house with window boxes bursting with red geraniums and surrounded by the proverbial white picket fence. Once upon a time, wrapped in a passionate, secret affair, Steve and I had not been white-picket-fence kinds of people, but here we were almost ten years later and all our dreams had come true: barbecues with our boys, picnics on the beach, afternoon games of wiffle ball and badminton, evening s'mores around a sparking fire, nightly walks down cobblestone streets. We'd even captured our sun-kissed cheeks and joy in a series of family photos on the beach—photos that would later take on a significance to me I could not then imagine. It had easily been the best summer of my life, and when it came time to return home to our turn-of-the-century farmhouse so Brett could start back at school, I was sorry to see it end.

We'd come home last week, and I'd felt a bit of a post-vacation letdown. But then, just last night, Steve had called to say he was forgoing his Monday night cigar dinner with his old friends at the golf club. "I'm coming home early," he'd said with a touch of mischief in his voice; apparently, he, too, hadn't been ready to settle down into our usual domestic routine of dinner, cleanup, and bedtime for the kids, then a quick conversation in our own bed before lights out. Still infected with the magic of summer, I'd greeted my husband's early return with the passion of a woman welcoming her soldier back from war—an urgency unusual after ten years of coupledom—and we'd ended our intimate evening by making love in front of the fireplace.

Not, of course, the usual nightcap for parents of small children.

Now, as I pulled up to the house and unfastened Colton from his car seat, I laughed at myself a bit for the way I still felt like I was walking on air this morning, as if I had just tumbled into love as I had many years before.

I heard the phone ringing inside the house and hurried inside, Colton on my hip, his sleepy head against my shoulder. Slightly breathless, I answered it. The clock near the phone read just after 8:45 a.m.

"It's me." It was Steve. "I just wanted to call and thank you for last night and tell you how much I love you."

What did I say in reply? His words stand out as though preserved in amber, while mine, years later, float away from memory like fallen leaves in the slow current of a river. Surely, I said, "I love you too," perhaps rhapsodizing a bit about how happy I was that morning, almost conspicuously so; I wondered if the other parents dropping off their kids at school had noticed me grinning and given me strange looks.

In any case, we hung up. The day felt even more shimmering, even more amplified, after Steve's call. I loved and was loved, the true fairy tale.

Did I resolve to keep days like this in mind when I was frustrated over workmen taking longer than promised, when dealing with miscommunications with my stepson's mother, when speaking to my own mother on the phone and conversations became charged? Perhaps I should have, but in truth, although I didn't take my happiness for granted, it had become a lucky given in my life, an insulator from petty frustrations, and in that moment—bouncing my second child on my hip, standing in the middle of our home—I don't recall taking any time to consider difficulties that seemed far away. Our dream house was still being built. The problems I'd faced at other stages of my life no longer felt as enormous as they once had, and although I was a wife and mother, I was still young enough to believe, in an unspoken way, that this was how things were meant to be. You grew up and found love and had a family and—*poof!*—the demons of the past melted away like so much winter slush washed away by the first strong sunshine of spring. This was my happily ever after, just like little girls everywhere are trained to believe. "The End" was flashing on the screen, the credits rolling. This was my life, and though I could hardly believe it, I expected that now that I'd found it, things would remain this way indefinitely—maybe even forever, until someday Steve and I, elderly and surrounded by our sons and grandchildren, would die of old age together, peacefully, in our sleep. Together until the last breath.

The phone rang again. It was Kenny, our neighbor and close friend. He spoke right over my cheery hello, blurting, "Tell me Steve's there. Tell me he's at home."

"Steve's at work," I said, confused. "He left at four thirty this morning just like he always does."

"I'm on my way over," Kenny said urgently, his voice shaking. "Turn on the TV."

My feet moved on autopilot, a pit of dread opening in my abdomen, and I rushed from the kitchen to the family room to switch on the television, Colton fussing a bit now on my hip. Kenny and his wife, Laura, shared a driveway with Steve and me, so by the time I'd flipped the TV on, he was standing in the doorway. My stomach rumbled loudly, like a warning.

I don't know what I expected—perhaps that Kenny would stride to the television and flip to whatever channel he was instructing me to view—but instantly I realized that wouldn't be necessary. Kenny and I stood side by side, watching one of what would be seemingly millions of replays: a lone airplane flying directly into one of Manhattan's Twin Towers.

Kenny swept Colton from my arms as I sank to the floor.

On the television, people were talking in panicked, stunned, and halting voices. "A commuter plane," I heard a newscaster say, shocked. Steve worked as an equity stockbroker at the Cantor Fitzgerald offices, on the 104th floor. The plane had flown into the building a few floors below them.

I heard myself saying, "I need to call my father."

Kenny gave me the phone. And then I was, in fact, talking to my father, my words a jumble of terror and denial.

"It's okay," he was saying when, on our respective television screens, the second plane hit the South Tower, a burst of smoke and flames.

Kenny, my father, and I all screamed.

And in one instant, it seemed clear that nothing would ever be okay again. A hole had opened in the world and I was standing inside it, about to be swallowed up.

I had barely hung up with my father when the phone shrilled again. David. My brother, my rock, my best friend. "I'm on my way," he said simply.

By now, neighbors and families were beginning, unbidden, to arrive. Kenny was fielding the front door.

Though we'd only lived there for five years, Steve and I were already integrated into our community. Part of what I loved about Steve was how much he cared about other people, how easily he fit into any group and made everyone feel welcome with his easy warmth. Kenny, who was a plumber, had told me in the past that Steve wouldn't treat him any differently if he were the CEO of a Fortune 500 company, and I knew from experience that this was true. Although Steve was successful and came from a privileged family, he never judged others by their bank accounts or superficial achievements. He could look through that outside noise and see goodness inside—he'd not only done as much in my presence with others, he had also done it with *me*. Neither of us had been our best selves when we'd met, and yet somehow we'd seen through to the other's potential—to our potential together—until our vision had come true. That vision was suddenly in flames, and with it, hope.

Within an hour, the house was crowded with people. I can still see them there, that gaggle of bodies that served as my lifeline two decades ago, some of whom are no longer living. They come to me in flashes: arriving, not saying much, feeding Colton his bottle, asking if I need anything. Two of my three brothers arrived in turn—first Sandy, my youngest brother, a big and burly ex-Marine who looked tough but was the emotional softie of our family. Then David arrived, enveloping me into a tight embrace that I never wanted to end. I clung to them both, desperate to believe that if they were here, nothing could hurt me. My brothers had always been my protectors, and I couldn't stand the thought of letting them out of my sight—my talismans against the surreal horrors on the TV that kept spooling the same horrifying footage over and over again. My eldest brother, Scott, had already embarked on the four-hour drive from Massachusetts to make it to my side.

Four hours. Surely by then Steve would be home and this would all be some insane misunderstanding; surely by then everything would be fine.

Surely, he had gotten out of the tower and just hadn't been able to reach me yet.

Around me in the house, people screamed and wept, but I couldn't shed a tear. No: Steve must have gone out—he had gone out to get some air, go for a walk, get a bagel or a coffee. It wasn't common for him to leave the trading desk, but then again it wasn't common, after ten years, for him to call me at 8:45 a.m., barely into his workday, to profess his love and speak in hushed tones about our beautiful and sexy night of lovemaking; it wasn't common for me to spend the drive home from Greenwich Catholic School marveling at the crisp, clear sky and blushing to myself in my car; it wasn't common for Steve to cancel his Monday night cigar dinner with his buddies, as though he knew he needed to be home—nothing about *any* of this was normal. Surely, Steve had gone for a walk, was right now too far from the buildings to know what was happening, was lost in thought about the strange but ordinary splendor of our lives, and any moment would call, shocked and devastated upon returning to work to find wreckage and mayhem but very much alive.

I slumped at the dining room table, shock and rage and disbelief radiating from my body like a force field.

Four of my girlfriends surrounded me and attempted to soothe me.

"I have to pick Brett up from school," I said—to nobody in particular, but they sprang into action, offered to go for me. I shook them off. "I need to be there to get him," I insisted, "or he'll wonder why I'm not there."

Although I did not believe Steve was dead, I must have looked frighteningly unhinged—one of my friends handed me a Valium and my closest friend, Cheryl, insisted on driving with me, probably worried that I would veer off the road and crash the car.

Cheryl and I had been friends for four years, an in-the-trenches friendship between two boy-moms. She was jovial, kind, with dirty blond hair and a kindred spirit I counted myself lucky to have found. She kept her arm tightly around me as we walked out to the car.

The last time I'd been in my Range Rover, only hours before, I'd been as happy as I could ever remember being. Now, the thought of that happiness felt obscene, a dream that had suddenly flipped into a nightmare.

The same sun I'd marveled at earlier was still shining, but now it felt too bright, almost offensive. It was only ten thirty or eleven in the morning—but the parking lot was full. It hadn't occurred to me, despite the fact that some fifteen people had shown up at my house, that of course everyone at school would know what happened in the city too. People I cared about, people with whom my children played, people I knew only vaguely and said hello to in the park. It was a small private school, and nobody was a stranger.

Cheryl and another friend, Diane, led me into the cool and strangely quiet hallways of the school because I seemed incapable of walking on my own. We opened the door to the gym; it was crowded with people, and yet the silence reverberated off the walls like an echo of nothingness. All eyes were on me, and in their transformed faces I saw the magnitude of what had happened.

My first sob broke through, and in the front lobby of the school, I fell to the ground. From there I dizzily saw my son—small and jubilant in his navy-blue uniform—racing toward me, a wide smile on his face.

"Mommy, we're getting out early today!"

The eyes of the entire school remained on us—not in an intrusive way, but as if to hold us up.

I knew I couldn't bring Brett home to a house full of people screaming and weeping with no explanation. With great effort, I forced myself to stand, to hug him, to put a smile on my face. "Hey, buddy," I said. "Let's go over there and have a talk."

We sat together under a maple tree, my blond-haired, bright-blue-eyed boy and me. I'd had three miscarriages before Brett, and he had been the answer to my prayers and dreams. My entire life I'd wanted to be a mother more than anything. And now I needed to do what mothers have done since the beginning of time: steel myself to function, to act normal, to not frighten my sweet, funny, always-happy child—my little buddy with whom I did almost everything.

"Bud," I said as the school community, congregating in the parking lot, looked on, "there was an accident at Daddy's office. We don't know yet what's going on, but we're going to go home and wait for him to call and pray for him to be okay."

"Okay, Mommy!" Brett said innocently, crushing my heart.

Until that moment, I hadn't even let myself think of what it would mean to me if Steve were really gone; suddenly, I was overwhelmed. But I knew I had to keep it together in this moment. I had years' worth of memories of Steve. Colton was only a baby, Brett merely six. Their father would be a photo in an album, a name on their mother's lips. It was unthinkable.

I forced my buckling legs to stand, to walk past the well-wishers and get in the back seat of the car with my son so Cheryl could drive us home.

We had been gone only a short while, but when we pulled onto our street, both sides were lined with cars and our driveway and front lawn had filled with people. The crowd was so overwhelming that for a moment I feared the media had arrived, but I quickly realized I was looking at supporters, not reporters. People composed themselves as I walked by, some hugging me, my son close—if bewildered—at my side.

Once we were indoors, Brett raced up to his room, and I thought it best to let him go. I didn't know what to say. I didn't want him to hear anything terrifying.

I didn't want to hear anything terrifying.

I stayed, though, among the crowd. I was afraid to be alone, frantically relieved they were there, as if they might act as a human buffer between myself and what was looming.

After about half an hour, Brett came trotting down the stairs holding a giant sheet of paper. On it, in big, brightly colored letters, he'd written WELCOME HOME DADDY, and drawn stick figures of himself and Steve beneath the words. Many of our friends broke into sobs as our son walked solemnly toward the front door and carefully taped the sign to the outside.

How do I describe the end of the world? How do I describe the things that, once seen, can never be unseen?

My stepson Jeremy called, heard my voice, and immediately started crying. He was fourteen and lived with his mother during the week but hadn't yet spoken to her about what was happening.

"What do I do?" he said, his voice achingly young despite his efforts to be mature.

"Come home," I said.

And so he did. An uncle drove him and his twelve-year-old brother, Peter, to our door, where they rallied around their younger brothers. Cheryl's husband took Brett to a toy store; Colton's diapers were changed. Enormous platters of food seemed to materialize from nowhere: deli trays, bagels, cheese and crackers, Danishes. Everyone seemed terribly invested in my eating something, but I had no appetite. All I could stomach was the wine that at least blurred the edges of things.

By midafternoon, the television was off entirely. No one could bear to see, one more time, the endless, terror-filled loop playing on every channel.

The sun lowered in the sky without word from Steve. Later, when people asked me who planned the candlelight vigil, I had no clue, though likely it was Cheryl. I remember Brett's small body at the center of the expansive circle, the lights of our candles against the dimming sky, Brett's voice pronouncing, "Please, God, bring my daddy home even if he has broken legs. I just want him home."

By then, Scott was there too. But nobody—nobody—could make everything okay.

The doctor who had delivered my sons arrived at 11:00 p.m., an unbidden house call. He sat in a chair, holding my hand and praying with me, trying to calm me down enough that I could rest. My stomach was empty, the wine and Valium useless at knocking me out. He must have given me a sleeping pill because I fell asleep in my marital bed, David and Scott on either side of me.

I must have slept soundly, because my brothers left sometime in the night for sleeping arrangements of their own, and for the briefest of moments when I opened my eyes the next morning I was disoriented, as though maybe none of it had transpired after all; it was all a bad dream. Then, the worst feeling I have ever known descended upon me: the memories, the clarity, a heavy wall descending. The wine and sedative out of my system, I knew what I had been unable to face the day before.

I did not want to get out of bed—under the cover of sleep, it had all ceased to be real. But my children were out there in the house somewhere and I had to rise.

When I went downstairs, people were already there, as though they'd never left. Maybe some hadn't. Although no one was screaming in horror anymore, something about the atmosphere echoed my own feelings of despair. A night had passed. There would be no more candlelight vigils and welcome home signs. For even amidst the shock and despair of the first day, there had been *hope*. Some convoluted explanation might still unfold. Now, with no call from any hospital, no word from any colleague, there could be no feasible reason my husband had been gone through the night. Only one explanation remained.

As the second day began, whatever frenetic will to believe the best that seizes people in moments of tragedy had drained out of our bodies.

My parents—still only in their early seventies, an attractive couple—arrived, and it was clear they'd evacuated their Naples, Florida, home in a rush because my mother's blond hair wasn't set and she wasn't wearing her signature pink lipstick.

I thought suddenly of my first job, what seemed like a million years ago, at Morgan Stanley, and answering the phone on my first day, chirping "Stanley Morgan" cheerfully into the phone, only to hear my father's chuckle—"Honey, it's Morgan Stanley." We'd taken the train together in the mornings to work, and sometimes I would fall asleep with my head on his shoulder. Every morning we went to the Radio City Diner in Manhattan to get our coffee and the best bialys in New York, steaming and fresh and always homemade. In the evenings we'd take the 5:26 train home together, too, and I often felt conscious of the other commuters whose faces we saw daily, looking at us with admiration or wistfulness at our closeness.

Then, after three years at Morgan Stanley, I'd moved to the city, and that period of my life, of being first and foremost somebody's daughter, had ended; I'd become an adult, getting coffee on my own while rushing to work. When my father put his arms around me now, I could remember the old way my head fit into the crook of his shoulder, and amidst the nostalgia and love something else rose in me: something like anger that my father and brothers had made me believe I was safe inside the circle of their embrace, but now my husband's building had collapsed in a sea of fire and rage and there was nothing, nothing anyone could do to keep Steve safe, to spare his four sons the pain of his murder that was already being claimed by terrorists, to rescue me from wanting to fall asleep forever and never wake up again.

My mind kept flashing back to the weekend. On Friday, Steve and I had attended the funeral of the mother of one of his best friends. On Saturday, we'd driven to New Jersey for a client party; our hotel room had been right next to Steve's partner at work—also his best friend—and his wife. The four of us had stayed up half the night drinking wine, eating pizza, telling stories, cracking jokes, singing songs, and laughing until our sides ached. Now, three days later, Steve and his friend were both gone.

On Sunday, Steve had played golf with Jeremy and Peter, and as we were driving home, he'd looked at me and said, "I have the weirdest feeling, but I feel like I'm saying things to you for the last time." And then, the night before he died, after we made love, he'd said, "Life doesn't get much better than this."

And he was right. He had seen, over the course of the long weekend, all the people he would have wanted to say goodbye to if he'd known that he was living his last days. I think perhaps he did know.

What I knew—and what I still know—is that he'd died a happy man, and that I had been happy with him. And now he was gone.

It was 5:00 p.m. when the head of Cantor Fitzgerald's Connecticut office, Barry McTiernan, arrived at my door. He knew Steve well—you work on a trading floor together, full of bodies pushed shoulder to shoulder, foot to foot, and voices rising in each other's ears, full of the mercurial rise and falls of markets and fortunes, and you get tight. I felt sorry for him as he stood, stooped with exhaustion and grief, at my door.

He wanted to tell me that the Connecticut office had been speaking to the New York office through squawk boxes when the first plane hit, and although the 104th floor had already been irreparably severed from any safe passageway out, of course they had not known that at the time. Steve had continued speaking to him, he told me, even after the impact.

"He was calm," Barry said, "so calm. He just said, 'We're in trouble and I'm trying to get all the young mothers to safety.'" Then, they were cut off.

No living person ever heard Steve's voice again.

Cantor Fitzgerald had no survivors.

CHAPTER 1
CASSEROLE DAYS

In those early hours and days after Steve's death, I felt everything and nothing at all, often moment to moment. When I felt numb, I'd find myself standing in the kitchen or sitting in the bedroom only to realize I'd been motionless—practically floating—for thirty minutes at a time. It was as if I believed that standing still might suspend time, or reverse it, and render all of this a catastrophic dream. But this was no dream; it was a living, breathing nightmare.

This unthinkable reality was only reinforced by the nonstop television footage of the planes hitting the towers, over and over again; newspaper photos of the many signs people had posted—have you seen this woman?—outside the World Trade Center; Manhattan covered in a wreckage of white ash that floated out beyond the borders of the island and over the water.

I woke up the next morning into a new reality. Still in shock, I walked down the stairs to the smell of coffee; the house, again, was already filled with my family and a few best friends. I was not alone, but I had never felt so lonesome and full of longing in my life. I opened the refrigerator to row after row of stacked casseroles covered by tight lids of aluminum foil, generous and loving pity gifts for which I had zero appetite. So many people had sent flowers, they filled every countertop. But I had no energy to acknowledge their beauty or, as days passed, and they drooped and then began to smell rotten, to toss them.

The initial aftermath of grief was an overwhelming blur, full of paperwork, financial details, and surreal conversations about memorials, all of which felt brutally absurd. Who could think about logistics when I kept imagining Steve's arms around me, only to feel the void of our too-large bed, the sheets on either side of my body cold to the touch? I wanted to float away, but instead was ruthlessly tethered to what needed to happen next.

And then, on one terrible afternoon, I found myself in Father Robert's office at St. Michael's, planning Steve's memorial.

Father Robert asked me questions, and I answered to the best of my ability about speakers and songs and when and where, but as weak light filtered through the stained glass window behind his desk, catching dust mites and spinning them in tiny, colorful tunnels in the air, I kept thinking to myself: *I am thirty-seven years old and my husband—the love of my life, my children's father—is dead.*

I prayed and prayed, but this reality pulsed inside me, as constant as my own heartbeat.

There was so little I could control, so little left to tether me to Steve, that like many grieving family members, the funeral began to take on epic proportions to me, akin to planning a wedding, as though Steve would be lingering somewhere, noting how much attention I'd paid to his send-off.

I convinced myself that I could show my love for him by doing everything just right. My funeral dress was perfection: a beige, light wool shift dress, trimmed in black, with brand-new high heels. How I fussed and struggled to find the right dress! And yet on the day of Steve's service I looked at it with disdain, knowing I would never wear it again after the smear of this day was trapped in it, like a bloodstain on the fabric. Defiantly, even though I'd had the dress altered, I left the sales tags on for what had seemed the Big Day, and as people embraced me, I felt those tags poking into my back. (Later I would return the flagrantly tailored dress, tags still intact, and be refunded my money. I wish now that I had donated the dress to someone in need, but at the time it seemed to me almost as though I could erase the day itself if I made a clean return; I could dupe the world, like the sales department at Saks Fifth Avenue, into my husband not being dead.)

I needed help even getting dressed that day. Thankfully, my best friend in the world, Gina, and my sister-in-law, Laney, were right by my side.

Gina and I had met while working at Morgan Stanley, where I'd worked right up until Brett was born—a decade of my life. Looking at her face, growing middle-aged like my own, I could still see the youthful twentysomething girls we'd once been, young working women in the city who never dreamed of such horror impacting either our personal lives or our beloved New York. Gina had been at a business meeting in New Jersey when the towers fell, and all transportation had been shut down to an extent that it had taken her two days to reach me. Now, she and Laney gave me half a Xanax, helped me into my stupidly splendid dress, carefully brushed and styled my hair, did my makeup (which on the one hand mattered not at all and on the other felt like a kind of necessary armor), and—over my protests—brought me a piece of toast, which they made sure I ate, although it tasted like sawdust in my mouth.

Then we were down the stairs and out the door.

When I saw my dad, his face drawn and somber, holding open the door of a sleek black limousine, I lost my breath. I sat down next to him and gripped his hand, thinking about the last time we'd sat side by side in a limo: in Naples, on my wedding day.

How could this be? How had we gotten from that glorious day to this hellish one?

The church was packed with hundreds of people who had gathered to remember Steve Cherry—*my* Steve, *my* love, with his good nature, his kind heart, his generosity of spirit, his uncanny ability to make instant connections that often turned into lifelong friendships. When Steve walked into the room, people noticed; he was warm and engaging and friendly, instantly setting others at ease. In his world, a stranger was never a stranger for long.

David—always steady, always holding me up—spoke first. He had officiated our wedding; now I was laying that same man's memory to rest. A nondenominational minister and former chaplain at West Point, my middle brother was not the holy type, but the way he looked at me and my boys with stricken eyes, his mouth trembling, felt like a holy moment, a sacred one. Here was a man who had loved me all my life, had loved my life with Steve, and would continue to love me and my children in the absence of their father, and the enormity of his own confusion, pain, and loss moved me to tears.

I was so deeply grateful for the support of my family and large community, and I knew not everyone was so lucky. Still, this did little in the moment to soothe the raw and hurting parts of me. I felt like my entire body was an exposed nerve; the slightest movement or look or feeling was painful, a shock to the system.

Many people rose to speak about Steve, and I listened hungrily, my heart aching. By invoking so many aspects of who he was as a person, by making Steve so *present*, they made his absence as thundering as any hymn. And yet I longed to hear others talk about him. I feared, already, the moment when they might stop. Once we stopped remembering him, then what? How would I fill all the spaces and moments beyond this space and this moment?

My stepsons—Jeremy, fourteen, and Peter, twelve—talked about the last time they had played golf together, just two days before Steve's death. Jeremy did most of the talking.

"Dad kept telling us how proud he was of us, about what fine men we were becoming, and great golfers too," Jeremy said, looking self-conscious to be praising himself in front of an audience. "It's hard to imagine that this would be the last time I talked to him."

I shuddered in recognition, thinking of all the larger-than-life gestures Steve had made in his last month or two of life, right down to calling me literally a few minutes before the first plane struck his tower. Although Jeremy and Peter looked so young and vulnerable, they fought hard to be brave, to show up for their dad in this most impossible scenario, and I wanted to tell them that their golf scores were the least of the reasons their dad was proud of the men they were becoming, no matter how much Steve loved golf. He would have been so proud of them in this moment, too, which sent a flash of anger from my heart to my throat. It was so unfair for these boys to lose their loving father, at their tender ages, in such a way. How could this be so?

Kenny spoke too. Haltingly, he said to the congregation, "I'm embarrassed to be up here—I'm just a plumber," and yet he went on to speak of how little Steve cared about income and status, and how he always treated everyone as an equal. I'll never forget Kenny's dignity as he stood there, and my sorrow that we live in a world where he felt any embarrassment at his trade or any doubt at his worthiness to speak before the group. He was our true friend, and I knew—and am thankful I told him many times—that he always had our utmost respect.

I found myself getting lost in the music until my body was attuned to it, and yet, strangely, I could suddenly no longer hear it; it was as if time and all my senses had been suspended and I had traveled somewhere else entirely. My memories of how Steve felt, smelled, and sounded were so present in my mind that it didn't seem right—in fact, it felt like a terrible movie or some kind of sick joke—to listen to people remembering him, to find myself smiling momentarily and almost turning next to me to elbow Steve and say, *Did you hear what he said?*, only to realize he would never sit beside me again. I felt like I was relearning this every moment. It was as if someone had snipped a piece of yarn in half and I was trying to put the pieces back together in my hands, full of disbelief that they had been severed, wondering why they wouldn't reattach.

At last Steve's eccentric and—though many people who knew Steve didn't realize it—famous father, Don Cherry, a singer who had been friends with the Rat Pack and had sung his hit song "Band of Gold" at our wedding, stood to speak at his son's funeral. It was surely the saddest song he would ever write but never sing.

In a strange way, Don's speaking echoed Kenny's, like opposite sides of a coin. No doubt Don would have traded all his fame and his colorful past to have his son alive and well.

It was an elegant, regal event, complete with the National Color Guard and the mournful, melodic sound of bagpipes. But who cared—who cared?

Death, as ever, was a great equalizer. No notoriety could inoculate us from the pain, and no status or money could make our grief more or less real. We were all in shock and dismay, together, that day. And yet even then I felt an awareness that for everyone who didn't share a home with Steve—for everyone but me and his four sons—this terrible loss would become somewhat abstract with time. We were the ones who'd lived with him, whether full- or part-time, and we were the ones who would now have to navigate our way to some strange new land without him.

A man had recently arrived at my door with Steve's dry cleaning: his suits, freshly pressed, sleeved in smooth plastic, that he would never wear again. I don't know if I took them upstairs or someone else did; I only couldn't bear to look at them, this fabric tailored specifically to his body, his beautiful body that I loved so much and that had disappeared—literally—overnight.

We didn't even have a body to bury.

Grief is a viper, a problem that the brain simply cannot solve, and as such it is wholly ruthless. When it gripped me the tightest, I could not always empathize with others and was not my best self. Even now, I remember with sadness the way, at the end of her stay at my home, my mother and I exchanged harsh words. She and my father had been with me for some time, and when she—who was in the early stages of what would turn out to be dementia—said she felt ignored, that no one was paying any attention to her, I turned on her and barked that maybe she'd better leave then, because this wasn't about her.

My father smoothed things out the best he could, and my mother—hurt, but also wanting to do what I needed, even if it meant not being there—complied and headed back to Naples. To my initial surprise, though, Dad stayed. Without his cooler head, I would not have been able to get through even half the necessary paperwork in the aftermath of the death of my family's primary breadwinner—our anchor, our rock—a death that also happened to be part of a national tragedy in which everyone felt they had personal stakes.

Panicked and shell-shocked Manhattanites moved off the island in droves, and our nation talked of war. But in my gutted home, I was just trying to keep some semblance of normalcy when absolutely nothing felt as though it would ever be normal again.

The funeral was over, and yet each day I fell into a cavernous maw of pain; it was as if every morning I was swallowed up in the mouth of the world, the reality of grief.

One thing no one prepares you for when someone dies is the way people ask a lot of inane and insensitive questions to fill the awkward hole tragedy leaves behind, and one I heard nearly every day was *How are you managing to lose so much weight?* I wanted to scream, *I'm on the Dead Husband Diet!*

Meanwhile, Brett returned to school. It hurt my heart to think of him there, missing his dad, trying to study, so young and so sad, yet he was valiantly trying to achieve normalcy too.

Time marched forward, with or without us. Colton hit new developmental milestones, which I celebrated one moment and sobbed over the next because Steve would never see it.

Eventually, even my father had to leave, to return to my mother, who needed him, and their life together.

Before he left, though, my father asked me to make a list of places Steve and I went most regularly and said he and I were going to visit them all, so that the next time I went it would never be the "first time" without Steve. Hearing him say this, it struck me, not for the first time, that one reason I had been able to choose such a loving husband was that my father was such an exceptionally caretaking and considerate man.

Dad and I went to—and cried at—many of Steve's and my favorite destinations around town, but in my memory, I see us most clearly at Siena's, the Italian restaurant where Steve and I were such regulars that, Steve being who he was, we had become close friends with the owners. When I gave birth to Colton, the owner had brought our favorite dishes to the hospital. Now it was my father and me ordering the penne alla vodka and a bottle of red wine, and despite the intensity of my love for my father and the substance of our talks as we traveled Steve's and my memory lane together, no food or wine tasted the same to me as it had in Steve's company.

Maybe this was what it would be like for the rest of my life: I would continue on, but the flavor would never fully return to my days. I told myself that if I could learn to bear it—if only that—I could live with the blandness.

Hard as it was to believe, it was only once everyone was gone—my house no longer overflowing with people, the uneaten casseroles scraped into the trash, the sympathy cards still unopened—that my grief intensified to the point of being unbearable. Yet I had no choice but to bear it. My friends and family had insulated me in ways I'd not even been fully conscious of, sharing memories and bearing witness, and though I thought I'd already hit bottom, in their absence I learned that it was possible to hurt even more. I had two young children but I felt one hundred years old, conscious only, every day I woke, of how long the daylight stretched out in front of me, how many hours I would have to make it through until I could finally fall back under the cloud of sleep. The minute I opened my eyes at the start of each day, I already wanted it to be over.

One small thing that made a huge difference in those first heavy hours of each morning: My friends had gifted me with a new coffeepot. Why was this so important? Because Steve always made the coffee before he went to work each morning, using a fancy machine he loved. In the days after Steve's death, I'd stood in front of that machine feeling utterly helpless and thinking, *I can't even make coffee anymore.* So a few friends had gotten rid of it and gotten me a simple one with a timer. Again, a small thing, but in those days, every moment of ease felt like a massive gift; any second when I wasn't faced with yet another reminder of what I had lost—even if it was just my thoughtful husband taking the time to make coffee before the sun was up—felt like a tiny victory.

I leaned on Jana, who had been our nanny when I went on bed rest with Colton and Brett was only five. Her own family was far away in the Czech Republic, and we increasingly relied on each other as surrogate family. I'd watch her in the kitchen, talking to Colton in Czech and preparing a bottle, her long, dark hair in a ponytail; I knew she was lonely, too, but she wasn't *broken* like I felt. At times I clung to her life force, her efficiency and good-natured spirit. Her sweet and sassy presence sustained me when it felt like work to crawl out of bed even for the sake of my sons.

If someone had offered me a bargain then in which I could have had every emotion removed from me, like an appendectomy of feelings, I would have taken the deal in a hot second. In those early weeks, platitudes like *It's better to have loved and lost than never to have loved at all* offended and sickened me. No sweet memories of my luminous years with Steve, or even my love for my beautiful sons, seemed equal to the agony of living each day in my own skin without my partner, without the man with whom I'd expected to spend the rest of my life. *Please, take all my feelings*, I begged God. I would mother my children based on what I knew a mother was *supposed* to feel and do, but I would be hollowed out, no more pain.

If only. If only.

My father and my grief counselor encouraged me to attend a grief group. I was the first to arrive to the basement of the Presbyterian church where the meetings were held and I started to get nervous as I waited, wondering if anyone else was going to show up. As I watched the door, a beautiful young blond woman pushed a double stroller past our dismal, grief-filled room, her stride confident, her outfit chic—a perfectly tied scarf and subtle but stylish shoes. I felt a stab of anger and envy as she passed—I had been a woman something like that once, such a short time ago, but now she seemed an alien species.

Imagine my surprise, then, when suddenly I saw her doubling back, peering into the room, and then maneuvering her double stroller through the door.

She approached the circle of chairs and took a seat. Up close, I saw that her face was scrubbed of makeup—that despite her perfect skin, her eyes were a bit puffy from crying. I knew straightaway that she was grieving, too, and I was drawn to her.

She introduced herself as Sophie. She blurted in her mellifluous French accent that her husband had been killed on 9/11, and I gasped aloud. He'd worked at another firm in the towers; no doubt he and Steve had sometimes passed one another in the lobby, ridden the elevators together.

I began to cry, and Sophie did too. Like me, she was now parenting two children—a three-year-old and a six-month-old—while trying to make sense of the unthinkable.

In that meeting, I would learn never to make assumptions about what it is to walk in someone else's shoes—even if those shoes are high-fashion Parisian heels. I had looked at Sophie and seen someone who couldn't possibly understand what I was going through, whereas, in reality, she understood it better than almost anyone else.

As Sophie and I got to know one another, which happened in a flash—our shared grief provided a shortcut to deep intimacy—we helped each other reenter the world in baby steps: lunch dates at which we grasped hands across the table and cried sometimes, but were at least out in the sun and air again.

Incentive to spend time with someone who knew exactly what I was feeling drove me to rise from bed and rejoin the living. Many times in those early days, Sophie told me that she would never marry again. I nodded; I understood. Who could possibly replace these remarkable men we had lost so brutally and tragically?

Of course, time's relentless march forward did not allow either of us to stand still forever, much as we first wanted to—Sophie not only eventually remarried but even went on to have more children. But in those initial weeks after 9/11, sometimes it felt like the two of us were floating on a sea of sadness together, each of us the lifeboat for the other. We clung to one another, wondering how we were to make sense of our new lives amid the emotional wreckage, and both believed surviving was all we could even hope to expect.

Luckily, and although we never would have believed it then, we were wrong about that. But just as grief makes decisions feel molasses-slow, the feeling that we would never get through it was as clear as the cleanest pane of glass.

In late October, when Steve had been dead only six weeks, his mother, Sharon, surprised me with a phone call from her home in Los Angeles.

"How about a night out in New York?" she asked—and it soon became clear she would not take no for an answer.

"Jana can watch the boys," she said confidently. "You need to get out."

Dinner and a show, she promised. This didn't sound fun at all, but neither did looking at all the ghouls and goblins and skeletons and scary pumpkins lurking in people's yards and making a mockery of death, or so it seemed. The air was growing colder, the nights growing darker more quickly, and although I was getting out of bed more often these days, I was still barely functioning. Maybe she was right?

Even if she was being pushy, the bottom line was that she was Steve's mother, and I didn't want to alienate or upset her. So I agreed to meet her and Steve's stepfather in the city.

The Peninsula Hotel on Fifth Avenue was predictably gleaming and fancy. Sharon was a former Miss America, and she and Terry, her fourth husband and a wealthy business owner, lived in the tony neighborhood of Bel-Air in Los Angeles, where the streets were lined with pillared mansions secured behind locked gates and high, perfectly trimmed hedges. I knew she was concerned that, with all Steve's sons living in Connecticut but her own son gone, she wouldn't see her grandchildren as much as she wanted to, and I hoped my effort at getting all done up and producing myself for a "night on the town" in which I had no interest would prove to her my good faith and that I would continue being her daughter in Steve's stead. My heart wasn't in it, but I forced my body to comply.

Making my way to Sharon and Terry's room, I was determined to be as cheerful as I could manage. I reminded myself that while I had lost my husband, Sharon had lost her son; she, too, was grieving. When I thought about losing one of my own children, a flame went up in my heart and I felt sick to my stomach. I understood innately that no matter how old Steve was, he was still her baby, and that his being an adult didn't lessen her pain. I owed the woman who had given birth to my husband a good face and a positive attitude, no matter how false it felt. After all, I was being treated to a fabulous dinner at a famous French restaurant, La Grenouille—known for its extraordinary food and extensive list of fine wines—and then a show. And for all her social graces and playing her cards close to her chest, surely Sharon felt about as much genuine interest in such things as I did right now and was trying to help me. I was determined to be gracious and grateful.

What I didn't expect was that Russ, Steve's stepbrother, would be there, greeting me alongside Sharon and Terry. I kept a smile on my face, but I was more than a little taken aback. Why hadn't Sharon mentioned that Russ would also be joining our group? It seemed so odd to me, and I had trouble dismissing the strange feeling I had in my gut.

I had only met Russ a few times, and the first time had been memorable—not in a positive way. Rather, our interaction had made me marvel at how well-adjusted Steve had turned out to be considering his unusual parents and their musical chairs of sometimes-questionable romantic partners.

It was Christmas, and Steve and I were in Bel-Air. When Russ—Terry's son—came to the door, he rang the doorbell. *Of his father's home.* Did he not have a key? He lived in LA. I wondered what kind of a fellow Terry could be if his own son was ringing the doorbell and then stretching out his hand to say "hello" in the stiff and formal way in which you might greet an attorney. Terry employed Russ in his lumber business, so it wasn't as though they were estranged; in fact, they worked together every day. And yet there was no affection, no expressions of love, no warmth.

I'd found this exchange—and both men involved in it—to be a bit chilling, and Terry's recent absence from Steve's funeral had only exacerbated my unease. Now I felt a cold and panicked feeling in my belly: Was it possible that Sharon was trying to *set me up* with Russ?

It seemed ludicrous, and I tried to dismiss the idea, but it stayed like a hook in my thoughts throughout the night.

Russ was very polite to me throughout the awkward dinner, and at the show, and our conversation was casual and easy. I decided to just roll with things and not assume anything bizarre; this was Steve's family, after all. Perhaps Sharon thought having Russ there would provide a chance for me to feel close to Steve vicariously. Perhaps Russ's missing his stepbrother had made him game to spend the evening with me. My grief, my loss of memory at how to interact in the normal world, was no doubt making me hypervigilant and paranoid.

Still, when we returned to the hotel, I felt relieved. I could drop my cheerful facade and shut the door and escape into my familiar bubble of sadness.

I had just gotten into my pajamas and climbed into bed, figuring I would do some crying in front of the television until I finally fell asleep, when the phone rang. I nearly didn't answer, but then considered that it might be Jana with some emergency about the boys and snatched at the receiver.

Instead, it was Russ, asking me if I wanted to go for a drink.

Abruptly, instead of once again worrying what his presence that night might mean, I thought: *Why the hell not?* I didn't know when I'd be back in the city—the city where I'd met and fallen in love with Steve. And I enjoyed being with people who'd known him well and understood the things I said about him; people who also had intimate memories of him. My big plans for the night had been hotel television and tears. Perhaps this was a better option, and life did not seem to be full of many options at all lately.

So, I threw on some jeans and a sweater and walked to the legendary Plaza Hotel.

The bar was beautiful and iconic, with perfectly polished bottles and dark mahogany tables—classic old New York.

At that time, you could still smoke inside bars. Russ, although I hadn't known it because of his strange formality around his parents, was a chain-smoker. He pulled out his pack of Reds and asked, "Do you mind if I have a cigarette?"

"I didn't know you smoked," I said, and then, because I was deep in the fog of pain and the night had been bizarre and I knew that no matter what I would wake up in the morning and Steve would still be gone, I asked, "Can I have one?"

I had never smoked a cigarette before—had never even wanted to. The first inhale made me cough, which made Russ chuckle a bit, and then it made me feel woozy, dizzy, almost free of all my burdens for a brief moment. My head spun, hurting less as it felt farther away from me, a balloon hovering above my body. I took another drag, and then another. I felt like a different version of myself—someone who was, at least for a brief moment, untethered from the great weight of grief.

Russ and I had a few cocktails, and we smoked cigarette after cigarette. Perhaps I wasn't a different person but rather a version of myself I had never considered: a chain-smoker ordering overpriced drinks in an anonymous hotel bar with a relative stranger with whom I also somehow shared a strange intimacy, talking raucously late into the night. An almost stranger who was related to the man I had loved with all my heart, mind, and body; the man of my life, the man who was gone forever. Someone who, for the moment at least, was making it safe for me to numb out, escape.

Russ, like Steve, was tall, dark, handsome, and—without the deadpan formality he maintained around his father—easy to be with. I suddenly felt a tender compassion for him when

I thought of my own father's warmth and what it must have been like to grow up with a man as chilly as his father. I liked seeing Russ more boisterous and relaxed. If anyone had looked at us for more than a moment, they would have thought we were old friends without a care in the world. Why not settle into that fantasy for a moment?

We closed down the bar and crossed the street as it started to rain—an October rain for sure, crisp and chilly, but still holding a bit of that sunshine summer feel that the air had held on the morning of September 11. Steam rose from the sidewalk, streetlights created bursts of light in the puddles, and the subway rumbled beneath us.

I thought of the last phone conversation I'd had with David, a week after Steve's death, when I'd felt neck-deep in the logistics that had me in business meetings with lawyers about wills and estates and all the rest that mattered so much but also didn't matter at all. I'd left one meeting abruptly after becoming overly emotional—I felt as if I were sinking in quicksand—and sat on a quiet stairwell looking out the window at the sky, which was blue and bright and offensive in its insistent beauty. How could the world still feel so beautiful, so full of possibility, when I felt so much despair and hopelessness? How dare the world carry on without Steve in it.

I called David, weeping. "I'm so afraid I just can't do this," I choked out. "I don't know how to go on." I meant it. I couldn't see the path. The sun was shining, but I could see no light.

"You have to listen to me," David said, "and you have to trust me. I know you, Mare. You're going to find a strength you never realized you have. And you *will* get through this."

That night, climbing into the hotel bed, the spell of being anything other than the grieving widow shattered, and I wondered how David could possibly be right.

CHAPTER 2
AND IT BEGINS

This is not a meet-cute story. A woman, twenty-five, who works in a male-dominated industry of numbers and negotiations on the trading floor, where voices are always raised and time never stops, is having a late lunch with another woman in the same business at the bar of Palio in Midtown Manhattan. The restaurant is cluttered with male bodies in suits, traders and hedge fund managers, secretaries and assistants and interns, all dressed in neutral colors in styles with clean and easy lines. There are few things lonelier, these two women and others like them know, than being constantly amidst a sea of men, day after day, hour after hour, only to return to one's solitary apartment in the evening to sleep alone (or perhaps occasionally with one of the de-suited bodies), and then to wake up the next morning and do it all again.

What is also true is that these women love what they do—the thrill and speed of it, the power, the pace. Still, in this testosterone sea, the few women cling to one another like lifeboats, sharing intimacies and frustrations and dreams—and yet even as they do so, their eyes are often on the door.

The year is 1990. Second-wave feminism is, if not dead, desperately out of fashion. On television, viewers watch the *unmarried women of* Thirtysomething *struggle to find partners and root for them not to end up that worst of all things: unchosen. Our women, at the bar of Palio, are not yet thirty-anything, are achingly young, pretty, fashionable, successful, and ambitious. And yet because they are women, of course they feel the current of pressure that runs like a fault line under their lives: Clocks are ticking.*

The women sip their white wine and pick at their salads. They talk about their male bosses, their male colleagues, their ex-boyfriends, the men they wish they could call ex-boyfriends. They cross and uncross their legs on the tall, awkward stools that are made, like everything in this world, for the length of male legs, not for theirs.

One of the women is named Cathy. Although this is a common name and therefore would make a good pseudonym, in fact it is her real name. The other woman is named Maryellen. She is a good Catholic girl, just like the name implies, and named after her grandmother; she is close to her father, the doted-upon baby sister of three older brothers. Her mother is her best friend. She has naturally blond hair and is something of a looker, though she doesn't know it. She is perpetually trying to lose five pounds. The last man with whom she was involved was a train wreck of epic proportions, and though she is good and rid of him now, the detritus of it all still clings to her, such that she feels like an old building in need of a good tuck-pointing.

Maryellen believed she would be married by now. But also, it is 1990. So what if she's not married! She is a liberated woman. Except that most of the men in this restaurant, as well as at her office at Morgan Stanley, are married—unlike her, instead of going home to takeout alone on the sofa, they are greeted by their wives and children. There are probably home-cooked meals involved. Or, if they don't go home to their wives or children, they disappear with a mistress, and their assistant sends flowers to the mistress and the wife the next day. It is, the entire endeavor— being twenty-five years old and turning heads and living surrounded by men and yet being fundamentally so alone—an irritating cliché, and for this reason, as well as reasons connected to the unfortunate ex-boyfriend, Maryellen has decided she is done dating men in her industry. Done! Never mind that men in her industry are the only men she ever meets, as she spends much of her life either at work or commuting to and from work. Who cares? She would rather be on her own than go through All That again.

It would be so easy to be a man. If there were thought bubbles floating above Maryellen's and Cathy's heads, they might say something like that. Or they might say, These stools should be a bit shorter. *Or they might say,* Next time, I'm ordering the burger, *even though the next time, they will both still eat a salad again.*

Cathy recognizes one of the two men at the table behind them. She turns to the men and casually says hello. "Steve," she says, "I'd like you to meet my friend Maryellen."

Steve leans forward, smiling, and shakes Maryellen's hand, and it is like an electric current just short-circuited the entire restaurant and the only light in the room is between the two of them and it is white-hot and running wild. The man's eyes are a blue that calls to mind painted buildings in coastal Morocco. He is not much older than she—perhaps thirty at most—and absurdly good-looking, which in Maryellen's experience rarely leads to anything good. Nonetheless, she can't stop herself from returning his warm smile, feeling the wattage of her own face ramping up in his presence.

THE ROAD TO YESTERDAY

The four exchange brief pleasantries, then they return to their own meals, pay their own checks, and leave Palio to return to their respective offices, separated by only one building.

Unbeknownst to Maryellen, on the way back to work, the dashing, too-handsome-for-anyone's-good Steve turns to his friend, to whom he has been complaining about his sad and stagnant marriage, and says, "Now why can't I be married to a woman like that*?"*

This is not a meet-cute story. For starters, its hero is married, even if unhappily so. And our heroine is not a princess sleeping on a pedestal of flowers in the forest, surrounded by woodland creatures, waiting for a prince's magic kiss; on the contrary, though not yet twenty-six, she is already weary of the world and of men. It is 1990, and this is Wall Street. There are no fairy tales on Wall Street. On Wall Street, everyone is the wolf.

When Steve, the man who would someday be my husband, called me on my work line within twenty-four hours of our first meeting, I was both flattered and, frankly, a little annoyed. We had barely exchanged two sentences at Palio, and although I had felt that unmistakable flush of my cheeks and drop of my stomach the minute we grasped hands, I had done nothing to make him think I was on the market to be anyone's mistress. I worked with (and for) twenty men on a trading floor; not only had I seen firsthand their after-hours partying while their wives were at home with the kids, I was also often called upon to send gifts to these wives as compensation for the fact that they were married to perpetual frat boys. I was also just as often called upon to send gifts to their mistresses. I made their clandestine travel arrangements. I saw their limousine bills. Infidelity, not uncommon in any industry, was endemic in this boys' playground. To say my guard was up would be putting it mildly.

"You're married," I told Steve, trying to make my voice quiet enough not to be overheard. Already it was a given that we knew dozens of people in common. Wall Street, like all intimate working worlds, is a small one. "I'm not going down that road."

"Please," he said—not in a way that suggested weakness, but optimism. There was so much hope in his voice as he made this request. "One drink. You know nothing about my story, or if you do it's not from me. I don't normally do this. There's just something about your eyes, your vibrant smile—I need to get to know you better."

I didn't say yes that time. I didn't say yes the time after that.

By today's standards, that Steve continued to call might be interpreted as "harassment" by some, though he was never anything but polite, respectful, and kind. From this distance, these decades later, we also seem barely more than children playing at grown-up life. To put it mildly: I did not feel harassed.

I felt interested, intrigued. And I felt *tempted*, which seemed even more dangerous.

When you are a woman, about to meet a man you want to impress, suddenly everything in your closet becomes unacceptable—an absolute waste of money and the time it took to pick it out. Maryellen stands in her bedroom, her go-to skirts and dresses and blouses strewn around the room as though lifted by a tornado, staring at herself in the full-length mirror. She has chosen, at last, a silk wrap-shirt of a deep plum and beige, a silk skirt of the same pattern, and high heels. She is still at that precipice where, upon waking in the mornings, no makeup and her hair up in a scrunchie, she looks no different than she did in college, and yet when she dressed like this she might be a femme fatale from an old film. She is trying on outfits like identities: "With this one, who will I be?" She wants to be her best self, her sexiest self, her most intelligent and entertaining self, all at the same time. This is a tall order for any outfit.

It is November 4. She and Steve plan to meet at Cafe Luxembourg, a charming, perhaps inappropriately romantic spot just around the corner from her cozy West Side apartment on 71st Street, off Columbus Avenue. The restaurant is famous for its regulars, its friendly and knowledgeable bartenders, and it's on her home turf, where she feels she can control things. But the minute she looks at Steve, flushed from the chill of the air, with those eyes that make him look as though he's perpetually under a spotlight, she knows she's gone.

Cafe Luxembourg is also famous for the hard-boiled eggs on the bar, but Maryellen is a roiling mixture of excitement and nerves that makes it impossible to eat. She's sworn to both Steve and herself that this is going to be a "one drink" event, but the moment they begin talking, she knows she's tumbled into a feeling from which there is no escape. His last name, he tells her, is Cherry, and she begins giggling like a teenager.

"Mine is Pitt!" she chokes out. "What are the chances?"

Although Steve is slightly older, a married father of two, this coincidence delights him, too, makes them both feel as though somehow their transgression of society's rules is fated.

Maryellen forgets to be nervous. It is fate. What can she do?

Steve asks her questions about herself, seems eager to know her better, and immediately this separates him from many of the men with whom she works, as well as those she's dated, who could talk about themselves for a year or ten straight without noticing they hadn't asked a woman a single question about her own life. Steve Cherry is, she can tell right away, sincerely interested *in people. Is he interested in people, period—or is he interested in her? If the answer is* both, *how much does she stand out from the crowd? She doesn't know the answers to these things yet, but she wants to, and that scares her.*

What is there to say about the conversation of a couple already in the process of falling in love? That they talk about their upbringings, their love for their families, their fondness for children? That they both believe things happen for a reason, and this, this right here, between them, feels like proof of this belief? It would all be almost too perfect, except that some of the very things that draw them together seem destined to drive them apart.

"How can I leave my marriage?" *Steve wonders to Maryellen aloud.* "My sons are so young, and they're everything to me."

Maryellen didn't expect this drink to entail her date being so forthcoming about his marital dilemmas, but he is spreading it all out here on the bar: his engagement at the age of twenty-one to a woman a couple of years older who gave him an ultimatum he foolishly took.

"We got into a huge fight on the way to our own wedding reception," *he tells her.* "I'd kissed the wrong mother first." *The fights continued, and immediately.* "On our honeymoon, we spent a night in separate beds." *And their differences only escalated once they were setting up house, starting a family. Steve's beloved brother is gay, and his wife refuses to let him enter their* home, thinking he will give their children AIDS. Steve puts his head in his hands at this, from pain, from embarrassment.

Maryellen can't help but wonder, How has he gotten himself into this situation?

But as he talks, she realizes that marrying a woman with whom he had so little in common was part of a period of Steve's life in which he seemingly gave the reins of his future over to others in every aspect of life. Not much of an enthusiastic scholar, he went to the University of Las Vegas, where he palled around with his musician father, took up with a girlfriend, and made music himself, generally having a high old time, until his mother, Sharon, arrived at his doorstep and announced, "You're coming home, young man."

And so, Steve went.

Sharon was married to husband number three then, the chairman of EF Hutton. Upon her request, her husband got Steve a job on the floor of the New York Stock Exchange, where he's been in some capacity ever since. Back then, he was the only one on the trading floor with longer hair and cowboy boots, and though he looks the Wall Street part now, he still plays guitar and sings, he tells Maryellen. "Rebel without a backbone," he jokes about himself.

But Maryellen sees something steely in him, something irrevocably him even if he's been letting this first part of his life be dictated by the mandates of others. She has never been around a man who possesses such an obvious capacity for joy and celebration and yet also seems so palpably sad. He has made a series of wrong turns, and now he seems to have reached a dead end. He thought he could do his duty and live with his choices, if only for his children, but it is just now starting to dawn on him how young thirty really is—how many years he has yet to live inside someone else's ill-fitting skin. The choices are impossible, and yet when he looks at Maryellen, his eyes are alight, transfixed, full of (no question about it now) infatuation and desire.

An older couple next to Maryellen and Steve at the bar look over and say, "What a happy pair you two seem like! How long have you been together?"

Maryellen and Steve laugh and at the same time announce, "It's our first date!"—but under the laughter, the undertow of sadness pulls.

Now what? Now what?

When he walks her home, he asks if he can come upstairs, but Maryellen somehow stands firm, permits nothing more than a goodbye kiss. It is the best kiss of her life. It is the kind of kiss that she would exchange any sex she has ever had for without having to take a moment to consider. She will remember the first impact of Steve's lips on hers for the rest of her life. She thinks, *Movie kisses will look boring from now on,* and three decades later, she will still be right.

"I've just met the man of my dreams," I told my mother on the phone once my heartbeat calmed down and I regained my breath enough to talk. By then, Steve must have been two blocks away, and already I regretted making him go.

"There's only one problem," I told Mom. "He's married."

My mother at this time was still years away from dementia: She was my keeper of secrets, my closest confidante, my Person.

"I don't want you to get hurt," she told me. "But I trust you to do what's right for you."

In the course of a few hours, however, I no longer had any idea what that was. What if I never saw Steve Cherry again? And also . . . what if I did?

CHAPTER 3
EXPECT THE UNEXPECTED

About four months after Steve's death, I got an unexpected call from my lawyer.

"I need to give you something," he said. His voice sounded strange.

Hours later I sat in his office, weirdly nervous because he seemed agitated.

I reached for the package and opened it slowly. When I saw what was inside, I recoiled as if he'd handed me a hot coal or a live animal. "I can't believe it," I blurted. "How? How is this possible?"

It was Steve's laminated Cantor Fitzgerald ID, completely intact. There was my beloved's face, shining out from beneath the plastic, as gorgeous as it had been on the last day he wore it.

"How is it possible that *this* survives?" I asked the lawyer, who shook his head. He knew as well as I did that there had been no body, no remains.

I wandered out of the office, Steve's ID safely tucked in my purse, as if in a waking dream. During the last four months I had been plagued by nightmares. Like many who lost loved ones on that day, I'd watched the footage of people leaping through the windows of the buildings over and over again, searching for someone I knew. And of course I was also searching for Steve—zooming in, zooming out, all the while holding my breath and feeling my heart pound in my chest—clinging to the idea that I might be able to witness his last moments and also hoping I'd see no sign of him. I couldn't stop imagining the smoke and the flames and the horror. The sounds and images kept looping in my head. And I obsessed about the people I watched jumping: When did they decide to jump? Did they suffer terribly, or was it over in a flash? Did they think they had a better chance of survival if they jumped? I desperately wanted to know the truth, but I was also afraid to know it.

I decided to talk to the firemen who were close to the site, and I wonder now how many widows, mothers and fathers, sons and daughters, and uncles and aunts and cousins came to ask the same question: *Did they suffer?*

The firemen—many of whom would later lose their lives from health conditions they acquired while working at the site—told me what I needed to hear, and what I believe to be true: "I promise you that he didn't suffer. The smoke took everybody away. There wasn't enough time for pain and suffering."

I tried to let their words sink in, tried to let them soothe what couldn't be soothed, and tried to put the images out of my mind, although I knew that every year these same scenes of the towers falling and people jumping would play on the anniversary. I had to reconcile myself to the fact that a national collective grief would always remind me of my family's singular loss.

On the morning of Halloween, I literally could not get out of bed. I called Cheryl and asked if she could come and help me with the boys, get Brett to school. I was too weak to do it, and not merely with sadness; I had lost a frightening amount of weight.

After dropping Brett off, Cheryl took me to my doctor, Joel Evans, the same one who had prayed with me on the night of 9/11. Now, he sat across from me, held my hands, and said, "You need to eat half of a sandwich while you sit here, or I'm going to have to admit you to the hospital."

The best I can say is that I managed. But one half-sandwich cannot undo almost two months of self neglect, of self-punishment at the gall of still being alive.

That night, Jana had to take my sons trick-or-treating, as I was stuck in bed. I would say this broke my heart—and it did—but my heart was already in so many pieces that who was keeping track?

After that first solo trip to New York City, there were so many challenges that extended beyond the obvious constant awareness that my sons had lost their father and I had lost my soulmate. For starters, our small, tight-knit community, which had seemed like such a treasure prior to Steve's death and even in the immediate aftermath of 9/11, soon came to feel like a prison. Everyone knew everyone, and therefore, every single place I went, people stared. They were all either at a loss for words, acting too falsely cheerful in an effort to seem "ordinary," or—was it better or worse?—they asked the dreaded question: "How are you doing?" I knew our community genuinely cared and felt concerned about us, but no amount of reminding myself of my outstanding "support system" could keep me from wanting to snap, *How the fuck do you think I'm doing?*

I loved my boys, my friends, my brothers, my parents, but nothing could quell the immense dread and mounting agitation inside me. Although, after my Halloween visit to Dr. Evans, I had forced myself through the stage of grief where I could barely rise from bed, still, I hated drop-off at school; I hated Mommy and Me classes with little Colton; I hated going to the grocery store; I hated pulling into my driveway, where Steve's black Land Rover would never be parked again.

More than anything else, I hated turning on the TV. At first, of course, live coverage of the Twin Towers going down, of desperate people jumping to their deaths, was all that could be seen on almost any channel except those with cartoons. But even after time passed, the story continued as the dead were found in the rubble, as mourners tried to identify their family members' bodies, as the nation spoke of war and my feelings—an amplified version of the country's as a whole—oscillated. On the one hand, I craved revenge. I wanted to hurt anyone who had been responsible for 9/11 with my own bare hands. On the other hand, no vengeance could bring my husband or any of the departed back, and the loss of more American lives in a war with terrorism—a concept without any clear territory—was no salve.

Sweet Brett, whose heart was free of the rage simmering in mine, created a memorial spot for Steve in our yard. He took two popsicle sticks, made a cross, and painted the sticks, mounting a tiny picture of his dad in the middle. Every morning before heading off to school, he knelt down before this cross, put his hands together, and prayed for his daddy. As he prayed, I prayed too: for the strength to be an adequate mother to my children in the aftermath of this horror that was eating me from within.

More often than not, after his prayer, when Brett climbed into the car and buckled in for the drive to school, he'd ask me to play "Dad's CD." Three months before he died, Steve had recorded an album of original songs—love songs, in fact, and all written for me—at a studio in Nashville. I loved to imagine him there, with headphones on, sitting on a stool in the studio, surrounded by the musical dreams that the city inspires. This had always been his particular dream, of course: to be a musician.

I slipped the CD in, and as Steve's layered, melodic voice rose and fell through the car, Brett hummed along and looked out the window. He never saw the tears on my cheeks, and of course he couldn't know about the first time I heard some of the early versions of those songs: while I was cooking for Steve in my New York City apartment in the early days of our courtship. His voice on the CD, remixed professionally, swelled in the car like a perfectly timed wave, as if invoking his living presence in the small space. And not just his presence but also memories from our life together before we had a family. I remembered the stops and starts when he was first working on the songs, and his voice calling out to me, "Did you like that line?" while dinner simmered and I popped the cork on a bottle of wine. Listening to those same songs now, then and now became layered, as time often does when the person we love is gone from the world but their presence remains. It was as if I could feel every word in the beat of my heart as he sang himself back to me.

Meanwhile, even as I tried to normalize what was far from normal—but simply heartbreaking—my litany of despised daily activities continued. I outright detested cooking dinner. My pre-dinner ritual—vodka tonics with extra lime with my hubby—would never return. The easy marital rapport of chatting as we cooked and ate was gone. Now it was only me, plastering a smile on my face for Brett's benefit, feeling like an actress on a stage who'd been handed a calamitous note just before the curtain rose. I smiled until my face hurt, but even so I felt my sons were being deprived not only of their father but also of the woman I'd been when he was alive—the mother whose joy was genuine, who looked forward to our days together and tended them with excitement. In her place now existed this Stepford Mother who was going through the motions, and though the boys were still young, I couldn't help but fear my overwhelming sadness and simmering anger would contaminate them. Of course, my family was constantly there for me, as were my friends, holding me in a net of love and support, but they also had their lives to live, their families to care for, and their jobs to do.

There was a particular pocket of time, most nights after dinner, when my loneliness nearly overwhelmed me. If I hadn't had two kids, I might have sunk to my knees and just stayed there. But I reminded myself of David's words—that I would find a way to go on. Hadn't Russ and Sharon flown all the way to New York City to show us exactly this too: that they were still family and would be there for us, no matter what? My boys and I were not so adrift, I told myself.

But as I stood washing dishes after dinner, scraping the remnants of the chicken nuggets off the pan or tipping leftover macaroni and cheese into Tupperware containers, my body felt too loose, too open—a vessel of loneliness waiting to be filled with sounds and connection I knew I would never have again.

Sometimes I stopped washing the dishes, stopped scraping the food, stopped moving back and forth between refrigerator and drawers, and let the hot water run into the sink and over my hands until my skin grew so red that I abruptly turned off the faucet, and it was then I noticed the most dreadful sound of all: silence. The sky beyond the window held the deep darkness of approaching winter, the shadows of the trees dividing the lawn into shapes that resembled a shattered pane of glass.

I took a deep breath and returned to the task at hand. *Just keep going*, I told myself. *Do this, then this, and then this.* But at times the silence was so acute that if a tree branch happened to scrape the window, bent by a sudden gust of wind, I jumped from surprise.

Every once in a while, the dreadful silence was punctured by Jana, quietly singing a Czech lullaby to the boys upstairs. Even if I wrote my feelings in a million books as long as encyclopedias, it would be impossible to express my gratitude to Jana for her presence and support in those early months. There was only one of me, and it was hard to juggle two boys of such different ages and stages when I was barely functioning myself. Jana would stay home with Colton while I kept up with Brett's karate classes, soccer games, and playdates. Sometimes she offered to do the running around so that I could rest at home, but it actually helped me to stay in motion. Busyness was a distraction, a welcome one, and besides, Colton was still a baby and had no idea what was going on, while Brett's world had been rocked entirely off its axis.

Jana went above and beyond any "job requirements," spending as much time as she could with us, and this gave me the opportunity to give Brett days that were as ordinary, as comparable to his peers', as possible. And as I came to put Colton to bed, Jana might squeeze my shoulder as she left the room, her eyes as kind as ever, offering, "He's very sleepy," as if giving me permission to tend to myself.

What I couldn't explain to her, or anyone fully, was that knowing my sons needed and depended on me was all that was getting me through—that so-called "self-care" felt horrible in its solitary stillness. At bedtime, when I looked down at Colton's sleepy face—a face that bore no knowledge of what or whom he'd lost—I could already see Steve in his features. I wondered how many times a heart could split before it would never mend. Would I live the rest of my life with my heart as raw as a live wire? How would that work? How would the three of us live, find joy and meaning?

I pushed these thoughts from my mind and whispered, "Hi, guy," forcing a smile and leaning over to give Colton a kiss. He gave me a dreamy smile that set my heart in my mouth for a moment, and I smiled back. "We love you," I said, my voice thick but sincere.

It was in the ritualistic nature of my boys' bedtime routines that I found bits of comfort usually inaccessible to me. Colton first: bath, bottle, story—always *Goodnight Moon*. Oh, there was nothing like that smell of a freshly bathed little boy, bright blond hair just brushed. I held him so close and rocked him to soothing lullabies, feeling for just a few minutes like everything was right with the world. Then I laid him, innocent and trusting, into his crib. I always made sure that whoever put him down for the night—whether it was me, Jana, or a friend or family member—the last thing they said was, "Your daddy loves you very much and will always be with you." I knew Colton didn't understand these words yet, but I wanted him to know, as soon as he was old enough to process them, that there had never been a time he hadn't heard them as he fell into sleep.

Next was Brett's turn. Nightly, I would sit on the side of the tub as he splashed amongst the bubbles, talking about his day, about whoever was his new best friend. *Goodnight Moon* and *Madeline* were his favorite bedtime books, and reading him *Madeline* reminded me of my own youth and helped me escape for a small pocket of time into days when things had been simpler.

In an old house in Paris that was covered with vines . . .

Brett's bedtime routine always took a bit longer than his baby brother's; there was no leaving his room until he was fast asleep after having his back rubbed. Some nights took longer than others, but I loved every second. I wanted my boy to feel loved and—more importantly—safe. I made this vow early on after losing Steve. I would do my best to become a *survivor* of this horrific tragedy, not a victim, not a shelled-out version of my former self. I would live for our sons.

I wasn't there yet, but during bedtime routines, I began to envision a time when I would be. I began, during the tender nighttime rituals with our sons, to realize that whatever damage had been done to me on 9/11, unlike the towers themselves, I would not collapse. I was still standing, still capable of love, still capable of wonder and even happiness as I buried my head in the top of our sons' heads and sniffed. I was not dead.

I remembered, almost constantly, being told that the last words Steve had ever spoken to anyone still living was that he was going to find the young mothers and get them to safety. That had been an impossible task, and those women were dead now and would never see their children again. But that was who my husband had been—a man who wanted to return mothers to their children, and who would attempt to do so even as he understood his own life was in danger.

I was *here*. I was still with our children. I vowed that I would make Steve proud of all three of us.

Alone, this resolve to be a survivor was harder to find. Alone, my main impulse—when the hectic to and fro of the day was done—was to numb myself enough that sleep might be possible, that the moments between my children's bedtime and my own wouldn't feel like a waking nightmare. When both boys were sound asleep, their breathing soft and heavy, there fell on the house the suspended, careful quiet of sleeping children that adults tiptoe across as if it were a rickety wooden bridge, afraid to make a sudden move that might tip them out of their restful state. Does it make sense to say that I could not bear the fact that I no longer had anyone with whom to potentially *disrupt* this silence, that I would never again hold my finger to my lips and whisper, "Shhh," to my children's father?

And so, most nights, I grabbed a jacket, a bottle of wine, and a glass and made my way to the porch, where I might hear signs of nature (the hoot of an owl, the rustle of leaves in the tree) or signs of life from other homes (neighbors rolling their trash cans into the street, a stray bout of laughter through a temporarily open door). This was an even lonelier time than the after-dinner stillness, and as weeks wore into months and the many beloved friends who had tended to us increasingly returned to their routines, staying home with their families, it grew ever more intense. I didn't want to be alone with myself. And yet, here I was.

The late fall air was decidedly colder; gone was the fresh, bright feeling, like just-cut grass, that had still hung in the air on September 11. Time was moving on, which seemed both obvious and ridiculous. I wrapped my scarf more tightly around my neck and took a long sip of pinot noir. This time was so bittersweet: On the one hand, I had made it through another day; on the other, part of me didn't want to face another one. I didn't want to be without Steve—this was a thought I felt in every moment of each day—and yet loneliness had become my most familiar emotion. However unwanted, it was like a blanket I kept dragging around, desperately wanting to let it go but scared about what might happen if I did. If I didn't feel this gaping loss, this void, would I feel anything at all? Who would I be without this grief steering me around like a ship tossed off course?

Sitting in the porchlight with the darkness and chill of the street just beyond, my mind still sharper than I wished it were as I poured my second glass of wine, I inhaled deeply. Although the air was bitter cold, my breath seemed to burn my throat, reminding me of that feeling I'd had of being someone else in a different life, if only for a moment, when Russ and I sat smoking and drinking cocktails in a dark, oaky bar.

I lit a cigarette.

Once I stubbed out the cigarette, finished my last sip of wine, I would hover in my seat in a kind of numb stillness where my pain still sat next to me, but tamped down, as though a blanket had been thrown over its sharp edges. Now, I could half-totter up to bed and end the day, only to wake up the next and do it all again.

It would only be in retrospect that I realized how often I thought of Russ on those nights, like a flashing sign reading exit from the solitary pain I dragged with me like Jacob Marley's chain. Russ: a return to Steve's family, and also an escape. Even in his absence, this intoxicating combination beckoned.

Weekends were especially difficult, because my friends were home with their husbands and families and I felt isolated and on my own. One Sunday afternoon I was standing in the kitchen, and when I looked out the window I saw Brett outside in the yard, raking leaves in a slow and determined fury. He seemed so small, wielding a rake that was bigger than he was, earnestly and methodically collecting the leaves into a crunchy brown and yellow pile.

I opened the window and called out to him. "Honey, do you need any help?"

He looked up at me with his wide, open face, his cheeks flushed from the exertion, and with utter confidence and a hint of pride said, "I'm the man of the house now, Mom. I've got this."

The man of the house. My tiny boy, who should have had his father to look up to for another decade before any ideas of manhood even began to set in. Brett's determination was so sweet and sad that I couldn't even cry. Instead, I felt weightless, untethered, lost. With Steve, the future had felt like a wide and open space full of bright possibility, a place I liked to visit in my mind because it was full of children's milestones and summer travel and holidays, which were rapidly approaching. Now it was as if that space had been surrounded by barbed wire.

Thanksgiving came way too soon. *Please, God*, I prayed silently, *can't I skip it this year?* But, of course, I had to think about my children. I obsessed over memories of our Thanksgiving the year before, wanting that one back. We'd spent it at the home of our great friends Bo and Diane. Bo was a gourmet cook, always serving the finest wines. At one point Steve had been holding six-week-old Colton, who was wearing little brown cords, a white turtleneck, and a navy-blue vest, and I glanced over to see them just looking into each other's eyes. It was a moment so full of loving connection that I captured it on camera.

I would have preferred to sit staring at that photo all day rather than face the holiday. I would have preferred to just disappear.

Instead, Gina and I drove with the boys to Needham, Massachusetts, to spend a few days with her sister's family. Steve and I had been friends with them as well, of course, and they knew how difficult this would be for me—for all of us.

Gina and her sister Debbie tried their best to make it special and bought matching pj's for Brett, Colton, and Debbie's two boys. At this point in the game, all anyone cared about was keeping Brett busy, and it seemed to be working. But shortly before the big meal would be served at the beautifully set table, I felt a meltdown coming on.

Gina quickly ushered me into her car and just drove around the pretty neighborhood with me, putting zero pressure on me to be anything but the raw animal I felt like in that moment. I tried to focus on the bright leaves covering the yards and the brisk chill in the autumn air, but nothing could distract me enough not to break down, to succumb to feeling sorry for myself, my sons.

Gina understood, as she had always understood me. A beautifully laid table and new pajamas were no replacement for a husband, a father. She understood that beautiful things now came with hidden spikes, felt artificial, made me at times want to shout at those who believed in their power to save us from pain.

Eventually we returned, and the four kids were none the wiser. We went on with our artificial merriment, and I thought, *This is it. I have made it through my first holiday. It will be easier from now on*. But even as I told myself these words, I knew it was only more artifice. I did not believe my own lies.

After how challenging Thanksgiving was, I was relieved when Sharon offered to host the three of us at her home in Bel-Air for Christmas.

Steve was one of those people who had a Christmas spirit you could feel throughout the house. In the ghost town of my Christmases Past, a fresh-cut tree stood in the corner of our red living room—the bigger the better—with glowing lights and handmade ornaments. Lit-up reindeers stood outside on the lawn. We'd always taken our boys to the annual Santa time at the Stanwich Golf Club, laughingly enduring those early days when the boys would cry on Santa's lap and the photos would show them gape-mouthed and horrified before we swooped in to "rescue" them with kisses on their little faces. As years went on, the time on Santa's lap became longer as Brett read off his list of what he wanted or hoped for on Christmas morning. And to Steve, the more things that needed to be put together once the boys were asleep, the better! I would hear him laboring away gleefully and think, *This must be a guy thing*. Now *my* guy was gone.

I didn't relish the thought of our first flight since 9/11. Aviation security protocols had tightened and rendered airports more stressful than they had been before, not only because the security lines were longer and slower, with everyone learning the new rules, but also because we all shared a collective PTSD after watching those planes fly into the buildings only several months before. But I wasn't so much *afraid* of flying as I was livid, realizing that all of the brand-spanking-new security measures in place had been utterly absent in the past. These TSA agents, looking all high and mighty, were going to "keep us safe," and I wanted to say, *Fuck all of you! If you were doing this job before 9/11, my husband would still be alive. Don't you think you're going to pat me down without me having a mouthful for you.*

This is the thing about grieving that nobody tells you—the fury of it, the full-throttle, blinding fury, when everyone thinks you are supposed to be cowed and meek with your loss. I didn't feel meek but rather like a dragon breathing fire, as though there should be a sign around my neck warning, be careful, don't touch.

My son, however, was not angry but terrified. His father had been killed by a plane, and he was old enough to understand that all the passengers aboard had died too. I had to comfort him, assure him that such a thing was a fluke, less common than being hit by lightning. (Even so, this fear has stayed with Brett: When he was eighteen, flying to see his future wife in Portland, I sat with him at the tiny, informal Sun Valley airport and noticed him stalling even when the gate was about to close. Finally, he blurted, "I can't do it, Mom," and we went outside, sat on the sidewalk, and Brett, by then truly growing into a man in his own right, wept like a child. "How do I know that there isn't a terrorist on that plane?" he asked, and I had no answers; we both knew the question was not one that would be satisfied by a "rational" answer. There would never be an answer that could quell what had been taken from him.)

That December, though, as the year 2001 drew to a close, our plane rose above the Manhattan skyline, which I looked out upon through the window—the Twin Towers conspicuously absent, Ground Zero like the hole in my heart.

To see it from this far up, my boys by my side, I felt suddenly unmoored, as though I were leaving Steve behind—even though I knew he was no longer there.

We arrived in Los Angeles a few days before Christmas. My mother-in-law, the former beauty queen and then-and-future bride to powerful men, could be an intense woman, but she had loved Steve deeply and had clearly tried hard to make things special for us. As we pulled in through the gates of her Bel-Air home, I thought I had never seen so many white lights in my life. I truly think every tree was lit.

Inside was even more festive. Two seven-foot wooden nutcrackers met us at the door; garlands were draped everywhere. A roaring fire blazed in the fireplace, and champagne chilled in an ice bucket. Caviar sat alongside a perfect charcuterie board. And then there was the tree—the biggest one I'd ever seen indoors. Dozens and dozens of perfectly wrapped presents lay underneath. It all looked so perfect it was both touching and almost comedic. It *was* perfect, something out of a holiday movie, except for the one thing we all felt missing that no decorations or expensive feast could replace.

Christmas music blared on Sharon's sound system, and I silently hoped I wouldn't hear "I'll Be Home for Christmas"—still my least favorite holiday song all these years later. Mercifully, the music drifted on without that one stabbing me through the heart.

Naturally (or perhaps not as "naturally" as it would have seemed in my own family, given his relationship with his father), Russ joined us for all the holiday festivities. I found myself wondering briefly if he'd come because he knew the boys and I would be there, but then again, he was a lifelong bachelor—what else would he be doing on Christmas besides visiting an aging parent?

Even through my fugue of perpetual sadness, I had to admit that this all felt like a Hollywood dream version of Christmas. No snow, no chilly air, no icy roads, no need for heavy coats or wool hats. I was relieved to be in a landscape so different from the East Coast, where I had spent previous holidays with Steve. Brett found it funny to see statues of Santa Claus and Rudolph at the CVS when it was over seventy degrees, and I saw my sons blossoming in the sunshine, the change of scenery, and, more than anything else, Russ's presence. Throughout our stay, he was never far from Colton or Brett, offering to take them out.

Christmas Eve we all went to the Los Angeles Country Club for its annual dinner, and my boys swooned at all the elaborately decorated gingerbread houses. The staff dressed up as carolers, and Santa Claus and his elves were even there. I kept my focus on how happy Brett and Colton looked, their bright smiles a mother's perfect medicine. *I can do this*, I told myself over and over again, and unlike my Thanksgiving cry in Gina's car, I did.

And then, something magical happened.

At Sharon's on Christmas Eve Day, we decided to go to the balloon store. The plan was this: We would all write messages to Steve, attach them to the balloons, and then send them up to heaven.

That morning, we wrote our messages, tethered them carefully to the balloons, and stood watching our red and white balloons slip into the blue winter sky of Los Angeles, drifting up-up-up until they disappeared from view. *To you, my love, in heaven*, I thought as I watched them float away.

We then hopped in the car and headed into town to do some last-minute shopping.

When we returned to Sharon's, tired after a long day, bags full of presents yet to be wrapped, and parked the car, Brett suddenly caught sight of something and sprinted to the front door.

"Mom," he shouted, his voice full of surprise and wonder. "A balloon came back."

We ran ahead to join him; sure enough, one white balloon with a red string attached was hovering at the front door, as if waiting for us. Brett read aloud the message he'd attached—I miss you, daddy!—and as I blinked back tears, a powerful sense of comfort and safety fell over me like a warm blanket.

You remember us as we remember you, I thought, full of gratitude.

And this is why I believe in signs.

During this visit I began to see Russ in a new light. He wasn't as quiet and stoic as I'd experienced him in the past; in fact, he was boisterous, loving, and clearly enamored with the boys. Brett, especially, laughed more in his company than I'd seen since Steve died. I found the tightness in my chest loosening slightly, felt myself relaxing into sitting around the pool and soaking up the sunshine, knowing the boys were in good hands with this gentle man.

One evening after dinner, Russ even offered to put the boys to bed. I was afraid he would rush things, but soon I could hear him reading their favorite books we'd brought from home and adding his own touches to the previously immutable bedtime routines. As my sons' giggles rang through the house, something stilled inside me, tentatively unfurled.

About an hour later, Russ returned to the kitchen and opened a bottle of wine.

"Thanks for being so great with the boys," I said, and I meant it.

"They're amazing kids," he replied, and he smiled, which transformed his face in a way that surprised me.

In that moment, I scolded myself for having thought that his being a man of very few words meant he was a man of few emotions.

We sat for a bit in comfortable silence, until Russ finally said, "Well, good night," and left me to my thoughts.

I sat a few moments longer in the kitchen, sipping wine. Looking out at the spectacularly lit and meticulously landscaped lawn, I allowed myself, in the midst of my grief, a moment of gratitude for this family that had so graciously stepped in, and especially for Russ and his attention to the boys.

I was nonetheless taken aback when, the night before the boys and I headed back to Connecticut, Sharon suggested that Russ and I "get out like grown-ups" and offered to watch the boys.

Deep inside, this confirmed the suspicion I'd had since Russ had inexplicably shown up in New York: Steve's mother was trying to set me up with her other available (step)son.

I imagined this to be an attempt to keep us close, to prevent our drifting away somehow into whatever unimaginable New Life I might someday find that didn't center around her. Instead of being angry, I felt for her. I knew firsthand what it was like to lose Steve, and she had given birth to him, had known him longer than I had, and though their relationship had not always been an easy one, they had been close and loved one another profoundly. No doubt Sharon saw her son's face in her grandsons, just as I did. No doubt she worried that someday—I was only thirty-eight, after all—some other man with no connection to her family might swoop in and sweep me off my feet and it would be his family we shared holiday time with alongside mine. Steve's and my sons were far too young to have individual relationships with their grandmother yet, and it was all in my hands how much she would get to see them in the future.

I knew Sharon was a planner—I thought momentarily of the way she'd shown up at young Steve's door in Vegas, saying, *That's it, young man. Time to come home.* But although I found her behavior a bit preposterous—like something in an archaic royal family where a widowed princess marries the prince's brother—I also understood.

If only, I thought. If only it could be that simple. Here among Steve's family, in this familiar house, I felt closer to him than I did in the house he and I had shared, where his absence echoed around every corner. Here, close to his stepbrother and mother and stepfather, I felt part of his family in a way I didn't any longer at home. Though I thought Sharon's behavior more than a little transparent, I remembered how lifted from my grief I had felt with Russ in New York, however momentarily, and I was content, for one more night, to play along before returning home to the sounds of silence.

We went to the movies—*A Beautiful Mind* was playing—and had dinner afterward. We decided on simple burgers, after all the extravagance and elegance of Sharon's tastes.

We talked a lot about Steve, of course—the one link between us.

"I can't even begin to say how sorry I am, Maryellen," Russ said at one point. "I miss him so much, and I didn't even see him that often. I can barely imagine what it's like for you." I saw in Russ's face that these words weren't platitudes—that he did miss Steve, deeply—and it opened the floodgates of my tears. I cried, and he held me. But it was all perfectly platonic, Russ a complete gentleman—he seemed to have none of his stepmother's schemes in mind; he was just genuinely offering me comfort in our shared grief.

Once again, I was surprised by how comfortable I felt in his presence. And just as soon as I'd found myself weeping, I found myself having *fun*. At first this made me feel guilty, but I just as quickly let the guilt go. I knew, without a shred of doubt, that Steve *wanted* me to be happy—not just moment to moment, but for the rest of my life. Remembering that, I felt a kind of lightness, and for the first time since Kenny had called my home on September 11, something in me relaxed completely.

The minute I did, I realized how tightly wound I had been—how locked into a kind of emotional stiffness that literally hurt my muscles I had since Steve's death. It felt like my entire body had been in spasms for months.

After dinner, we went back to Sharon's and decided to light a fire and have a glass of wine, which turned into two glasses, then three. My body hummed. For so long, I had been surrounded by people who wanted to comfort me—who, yes, had loved Steve; *everybody* loved Steve—but couldn't give me the relief I needed. Here, with his own stepbrother, things were different. I wasn't just a grieving widow he was afraid to say the wrong thing around. Though his loss was not as acute as mine, he'd known Steve intimately, in the way only family can; here, for the first time, my grief felt like a collective thing rather than a burden I could only share with my poor little Brett, whose shoulders were too small for the immense load.

I felt for Russ's grief, and yet his pain freed me in some way, and between that and the wine and the prospect of getting on a plane the next day and disappearing three thousand miles away, I was feeling more unencumbered than I had in ages—a dangerous, reckless kind of buoyancy.

I also felt a little buzzed. The sensation was no stranger to me after all those months of drinking wine alone on my porch at night, but tonight, for the first time in months, I also felt like I could even touch the edge of happiness. I could see, perhaps, a part of that future I'd been afraid to even approach before now. I felt attracted to Russ, drawn to him, which surprised me, and also—even if only for a moment—made me aware for the first time that to survive deep grief was also to seek *life* in the face of it. It felt like I was learning how to be a person all over again, which meant I was ready to take action and not float in this state of *one foot in front of the other*, *chop wood and carry water*, and the other clichés I repeated to myself just to make it through the days one by one by one, like a game of the most depressing dominoes. Perhaps, I thought, it didn't need to be like that?

And so, when Russ stood up to leave, I clumsily leaned in to kiss him goodbye on the mouth. His surprise registered instantly, and I jerked back, muttered, "Oh my God, I'm so sorry! What was I thinking?"

Russ stood, tall and handsome, and as he held me at arm's length like a gentleman, I had to admit to myself that it was not *only* my grief that had urged me on. "You have nothing to be sorry for," he said, giving me a chaste hug. "I understand."

Did he, though? Surely, he thought my behavior motivated sheerly by wine, by loneliness... but was it?

My head swam—I wasn't sure myself. I was merely grateful that one of us was responsible enough to stop that kiss I would surely have regretted the next morning.

The actual next morning, Sharon brought me a cup of coffee as I was finishing up some last-minute packing and informed me that we'd be taking off for the airport in about thirty minutes. I expected that she had called us a car, but then heard someone enter through the front door.

It was Russ.

"I wanted to come to the airport to help you all get settled in safely," he said.

As he carried our bags downstairs to the car for us, I hung back, awkward as a schoolgirl after my forward behavior the night before.

Brett was ecstatic. "Uncle Russ! Uncle Russ is taking us!" It was wonderful to see him so delighted.

I knew Sharon would be delighted as well if she knew about my attempt to kiss her stepson (*Please, God, don't let Russ have told her*, I prayed), but I couldn't help but wonder if Russ thought the worse of me for it. Still, I was grateful yet again for his help. When traveling with two little boys, one ideally needs more than two hands.

But I've mastered doing it with just two, I reminded myself; I'd had to, and so I had. This was my new normal.

After saying my goodbyes—an awkward hug with Russ in which I made sure to keep my body arched far from his like the chaste widow I was supposed to be—I boarded the plane with Colton on my hip and Brett hanging on to my hand as I managed a diaper bag and stroller.

Unbeknownst to me, however, Russ was watching me retreat with his own heavy heart and secret sadness. Later, he would confess that he knew at that moment he "needed to step up and fill in for my stepbrother as best I could." Russell Mullin, a confirmed bachelor who at the age of forty-four had never wanted to be married, had already, seeing me and his nephews disappear into the chaos of LAX, changed his mind.

CHAPTER 4
MY YEAR OF LIVING DANGEROUSLY

On November 5, 1991, the night after I kissed Steve Cherry, a married man, good night in front of my adorable one-bedroom apartment on the Upper West Side and then called my mother, like the child I still in many ways was, to tell her I had met the man of my dreams, my phone rang so early in the morning that I was sure it could only be bad news.

Instead, it was Steve, up early enough to be sure to catch me at home, asking, "May I walk you to work?"

In my still-half-asleep state, defenses down, I immediately answered, "Yes."

It was a stunningly beautiful fall day, brisk and sunny—the kind of day I would, many years later, after losing Steve, come to despise. At that time, though, to twenty-five-year-old me, the day seemed sparkling with possibilities and extraordinary what-ifs, as did Steve himself, looking impossibly handsome as I glimpsed him striding toward my building, a cup of coffee in each hand. He gave one cup to me, and in that one gesture, perhaps even more so than in the stomach-dropping kiss the night before, we became a team. I accepted the cup, the warmth of it seeping into my hand, and Steve took my other hand as we began our walk, our warm palms touching in a way that was both erotic and sweet.

To get to work, we meandered slowly through Central Park, holding hands the whole way. I had the sudden thought that I wanted to hold hands with him every day for the rest of my life, and I only half-heartedly tried to push it away. That first day, I still had the presence of mind to be surprised that Steve would be so openly affectionate with me in public—wasn't he afraid we would be seen? That he would be caught? That people would gossip? But to say that Steve Cherry did not seem on edge or worried in any way at all would be an understatement. In only a matter of days, he had gone from being a man who believed that at just thirty years old most of the joy in his life was already over to someone intoxicated by the possibilities ahead, by the future—and it was clear he envisioned that future with me in it.

The change in him was visceral. While he'd been devastatingly attractive the afternoon when we'd first been introduced at Palio, he had not seemed *happy*, not exactly. I hadn't noticed at the time, because who on Wall Street looks happy? Stress and competition were our daily diets, and the effects of our job showed on our drawn faces and in our slumped postures and pensive expressions. Now, though, I saw what I had been missing. Steve exuded an uncontainable, almost boyish joy and enthusiasm that was nothing short of infectious—though I needed no infection, as I felt it, too, in the current that moved between us.

We floated through the park like teenagers who were falling in love for the first time. If anyone saw us together, the devil be damned. Caution was not part of our repertoire. We were too infatuated, too far gone. Although we had not yet slept together, it was clear to me that I was now having an affair with a married man—if not yet in the flesh, then absolutely in my heart.

The following week, as though my body were trying to save me from my own rash decisions, I fell sick with an awful cold. It's difficult, these years later, to access now how deeply depressed I felt, lying in my solitary bed, congested and feverish and lethargic and just really *sick*. I was madly in love; there was no denying it. But unlike when I went walking with Steve or when we sat together at the bar of Cafe Luxembourg, much less when we were kissing, my joy had evaporated and hard, cold reality, with all its warnings, was setting in: This perfect man, the most compelling man I'd ever met, was unavailable. He was married to another woman—unhappily, yes, but married still. I could not make a future of strolls through Central Park; I could not live on disposable coffee cups, however truly magical and electric it had felt when he handed that first one to me.

I was twenty-five! I wanted to marry someday—to have children and a family and a partnership with a man I would call my husband. Steve was already married, with two young boys. What was wrong with me? How could I snap out of it, forget Steve, and go about my life?

Grow up and regroup, I thought to myself between Tylenol-infused naps and sneezes into countless tissues.

Perhaps I could have talked myself out of my love haze during those long days languishing in sickness had Steve not been the epitome of thoughtfulness. Several flower arrangements were delivered while I was out from work, and Steve went out of his way to have homemade chicken soup delivered to me from some of my favorite restaurants in the neighborhood. He was, it was clear, a true romantic . . . but was the fact that we couldn't truly be together part of the romance? Were the obvious roadblocks against our future together, for him, part of the attraction? How could I know?

With each thoughtful gesture, I fell even more deeply in love and grew even more worried that I was setting myself up for the heartbreak of a lifetime. Being sick was one thing—it would inevitably end—but I worried that heartsickness I might be in for would flatten me.

The moment I felt better, Steve called to ask if he could take me out for a nice dinner since I'd been cooped up all week. After so much time to think, I was hesitant, demurred that I would have to get back to him.

Immediately, I called my mother and asked what I should do. I'll never forget her boisterously saying, "Honey, you never give up a free meal!" Her comment felt a bit like a tacit permission, and in fact years later my mother would admit that she knew instantly, from the way I sounded when I so much as mentioned Steve, how real my love was.

Her comment also made me laugh, and at least momentarily forget my anxieties.

I accepted Steve's invitation.

We met at Harry's New York Bar. I found myself watching Steve carefully for flaws, hoping for some crack that would knock some sense into me, but it quickly became clear that this was a useless endeavor. Instead, I kept thinking, *Damn!*

This guy really is perfect. In the warmly dark, sexy, and sophisticated Harry's, he had reserved a table for us in front of the roaring fire, and he ordered us a bottle of Chateau Montelena. At the time I knew nothing about wine, had no knowledge that this was to become "our" wine or that we would one day visit the vineyard together—I knew only that it was the finest red I had ever sipped. That night, I sat inside my young skin, aglow with attraction and adoration and about to sink into despair at the mess I was willfully getting myself into. I knew, without a shred of doubt, that I was a goner.

This time when Steve walked me home, I invited him upstairs. It would be a lie, of course, to say I couldn't have stopped myself. I had free will—I was conscious both of the fact that I was opening myself up to pain and that I was, by the doctrine of my faith and most laws of human decency, committing a sin, not only against Steve's individual wife (who, of course, in my entirely biased opinion, didn't sound like the kindest woman alive) but against *all* wives, everywhere, who expect and trust their husbands' fidelity. A well of complexity opened up within me—one I had never had to wrestle with before at my young age. If I sent Steve Cherry away, I would spend the rest of my life wondering what might have been. Wasn't that, too, a kind of crime, of a different, nonreligious sort? Wasn't it wrong in some deep way to see a chance at extraordinary happiness and turn away? What sort of system demands two people not over thirty years old to spend the rest of their lives bound by "duty," flatlining their own desires and emotions?

Were these only rationalizations? Of course they were. But as we walked up to the fourth floor of my old brownstone building, the butterflies in my stomach were flying hard and leading the way.

We sat close together on the couch. Steve lit the tiny fireplace with a Duraflame log, and the sparks flying from the too-small grate seemed an apt and undeniable metaphor for what was happening between us. We couldn't keep our hands or our mouths off of each other. I had never known this kind of obliterating passion, the kind that makes it impossible to even think—yet somehow, I found it in me to draw the line before we had sex. My own self-control surprised me. As Steve graciously accepted my boundaries, even though I knew he was as frantic with desire as I was, I found myself thankful that I knew, from our conversations about his marriage, that he and his wife no longer slept side by side. Had I believed I was sending him home to another woman's bed, I might not have had the strength to send him home at all.

I woke up the next day with my stomach still fluttering and my heart pounding like I'd just come back from a run. My workday could not end fast enough, as I knew Steve well enough by now to know I would see him once the day ended.

After the 4:30 p.m. bell rang and the trading day closed, there he was in the lobby, holding a large bag tied with a red ribbon. It was, to my amusement, a fire grate. "Now *this* is the size you need," he told me, to my amusement. "A quarter-cord of wood is being delivered tomorrow."

How—even now—can I explain that it was this, more than any fancy dinners or bouquets of flowers, that eviscerated my final vestiges of self-control completely? We couldn't get back to my apartment fast enough. Wine poured, fire lit, Bonnie Raitt crooning in the background . . . this time, there was no more confining us to the couch.

And so, my days as an Other Woman began. Every morning, Steve appeared at my door with two coffees and we made our way through Central Park to our respective offices, one block apart. I sometimes felt self-conscious walking down the street; our desire was so palpable that it made me feel vulnerable. But it also made me feel alive, turned all the way up, in a way I never had been before. I noticed the beauty in people passing by in a new way; I felt benevolent toward every stranger, alerted to every golden leaf catching the sunshine in the piles beneath the shedding trees.

Between our two offices was a bar called La Cite where my coworkers and I had long gone several nights a week after work for a quick drink. Now, it was where Steve and I sometimes met in the afternoons—and we were not above heavy make-out sessions in the spacious bathroom stalls of the women's room. (I had never been so glad to work in a male-dominated industry; the women's room was almost invariably utterly empty during the day!) From a distance, it's almost hard to believe our risqué antics were anything but reckless and a bit ridiculous, but at the time we were so driven by our desire for each other that we had lost the will to think straight. We spent the workweeks meeting up for dinners at romantic restaurants or cooking cozily in my apartment.

Sometimes, on those evenings at my place, Steve brought his guitar and strummed new songs he had written for me while I cooked. As the meat sizzled in the pan, I heard his sultry voice and felt it was a sound I had been waiting to hear all my life; to say that I felt about to swoon like some old-fashioned heroine of a romance novel would be accurate.

It wasn't just that I had a beautiful, charismatic man writing songs for me, heady and romantic as that was—it was that

Steve was *really good*! His voice was textured and versatile, by turns sweet and pure or complicated and layered. I didn't understand why his wife, who would not so much as allow Steve and the buddies he played with to practice in their family garage, had no patience for his passion for music. And what about his mother? His father had made a living at it, but she had fetched Steve from Las Vegas and dismissed his desires to follow in his father's professional footsteps. Perhaps she was worried he would follow in his father's interpersonal footsteps too?

But despite his polished veneer on Wall Street, his knowledge of fine wines and upscale restaurants, music was closer to the core of Steve's real identity than anything else. It was his passion, and what he was undoubtedly meant to do. As I became his biggest fan and encouraged him, he would go on to work with a voice coach and eventually hire a manager, making the Steve Cherry Band a reality at last.

Oh, the magic of those days. The paradox. The heat and the sweat. The thrill, as Steve's band began to play in hot little spots all over the city, gaining popularity, packing the house, young girls in the front row mooning over him, while I knew that many of his songs were written for me, that he was mine and I was his. And yet, of course, at the end of the night he would have to take the last train home to his family. The partings were brutal for us both, and we often stood on the platform kissing wildly, already disheveled from a long night out at a music venue or hours in my bed, wanting to stay together, trying to delay our parting.

Then Steve would board the train and ride home and both of us would sleep alone, counting the hours until we could be together again.

Winter was setting in.

Our love was flourishing, but being an Other Woman is, if not the high-water mark of my moral choices, also not for the faint of heart. Weekends were especially difficult. Not only was it harder for Steve to get away to the city on weekends, but of course he *wanted* to be with his sons, and I understood that absolutely. The boys were why he was staying in his marriage to begin with, as they were only two and four years old. They needed their father, and he loved them and treasured days with them. This, in fact, was a big part of why I loved him: his dedication to his children.

But on weekends, no matter how truly I believed that Steve loved me and only me romantically, with his heart and soul and especially his voice—no matter how convinced I was that he had checked out of his marriage, both emotionally and sexually, some time before we even met or became involved—I could no longer exist only in the cocoon of our affair. Steve had a family; he had sons. I spent my weekends in limbo, even when I was with my girlfriends or parents, waiting for his return, or what I saw as my "real life." But Steve's real life was decidedly split in two. Even though our affair was, among many who knew us both, a bit of an open secret, it did not change the fact that he lived elsewhere, kept house elsewhere, had children elsewhere, in a world where I did not even exist except in his memory and his anticipation.

It was December, the holiday season. I had lived, in only two scant months, an entire lifetime of love with Steve Cherry. But the longer we remained in this place of limbo and split lives, the longer I was closing myself off to the possibility of the life I deeply wanted to live with him in the light of day.

"I'm going to leave," Steve promised me often. "I just need to get through the holidays."

But would there ever be an ideal time to leave a marriage with two young children? What if, after Christmas, the goal post just got moved—and moved again? Would these months stretch into years? And if so, how long could I hold on to the fantasy before it would be time to go? I didn't want to be the cliché of the Other Woman; I knew I was *the* Woman and I wanted the reality of our lives to match this knowledge.

The annual Christmas party at the country club. Saturday night. A black-tie affair. An unhappily married man and woman, both dressed to the nines, dance together on a crowded dance floor for appearances, even though many of their friends suspect or know the truth of their situation. A band plays. What song plays while they dance?

In her one-bedroom apartment in the city, the man's young lover cannot hear the band, and she doesn't want to hear it anyway. She wants to hear her lover's voice, singing the songs he wrote for her, in the delicate dance of their evolving love for one another. Meanwhile, the man feels his wife's body in his arms, once so familiar but now almost as alien as their estrangement has grown. She does not love him either, whether or not she may think she does. She disdains his music, refuses his brother entry to their home, has grown as accustomed as he has to the fact that when they speak at all, they usually fight. Is this what she wants for her life? he wonders. Is she any happier than he is? How is any of this good for their children, whom they both love?

But, of course, he is a man, and there is much he doesn't understand about the stories with which his wife and all women their age grew up—the stories of home and hearth and children and the implications that the man to whom a woman is wed is what conveys her worth. That she is here in their town wearing her Wife Skin, her Mother Skin, while he is free in the city all day working, singing in clubs, snuggling in cozy nooks with his adoring lover or lying beneath her duvet with her, feet intertwined, laughing and satiated. He thinks about missing his sons if he were to leave, but he does not think of the fact that the world will process his leaving far differently than they would if his wife were the one with a twenty-five-year-old lover in the city, if his wife were the one on stages crooning songs instead of home with their boys.

It is the end of 1991. Many women have careers, of course—his lover is such a woman. He never told his wife she had to stay at home, never told her she had to be dependent upon him, never told her she had to make this world of country clubs and stay-at-home mothers and pointless acts for appearances the substance of her life. Other women have made other choices; she could too. He does not think of what the world might think of her if she made the choices he has made.

One year from now, Hillary Clinton will be widely castigated in the media because of a comment that she does not stay home and "bake cookies." This is a man's world. This man, raised by a powerful mother, does not think, as he prepares to end his marriage, of all the forces in the world that may have made his wife into the woman she is—of the fact that his lover is one of the few women in their profession, their world so male-centric that they can tear at each other's clothes in the women's room of La Cite in the middle of the day with nary a fear of being walked in upon. He certainly does not think of what the world would say about his wife, the mother of two young children, if she were the one sitting on a sink with her arms wrapped around a man's waist in the bathroom of a bar in downtown Manhattan. It is 1991; it will be years before thinking about such things will become a more common part of the vernacular, and by then this man will be dead, his life cut tragically short in its prime.

It is almost Christmas. The man thought to wait until the holidays are over, but feeling his wife's now strange-seeming body in his arms, he finds he cannot wait another night. In the eyes of his lover, this will make him a hero, a man of his word. In the eyes of his wife, this will make him the villain, the Enemy, forever. He has not even, quite yet, thought that far ahead, however; he has thought only of the time he will miss with his sons because of what he is about to do. He loves them more than life itself—loves them enough to die for them—but is it a favor to them to live unhappily in a loveless marriage, to present that as a model of how to live their best lives? Perhaps he has not thought that far either, exactly. He only knows what he wants and what he wants no longer. He only knows what he must do in order to be true to himself, and that, somehow, there must be virtue in that, in no longer living a lie and insisting upon Truth. There must be. He hopes fervently that there is.

He is quiet on the drive home from the country club, the sky dark and the road wintry and scattered with pockets of frozen snow, but his wife thinks little of this, as silence is a norm between them. When they arrive home, he asks her to go upstairs and change and meet him back downstairs; he says some variation of the cliché, We have to talk. Does his wife know, as she ascends the stairs, what he is about to say? That he cannot continue in this marriage for even one more day? Does she know that his mistress has been worrying herself sick that he will never leave, but all her *worry is for naught, because as it turns out he will move heaven and earth to be with her?*

In the end, it is his wife's head that rests on the chopping block. We will watch it roll away, with all the implications of a callous good riddance. Goodbye.

We look at this scene from the outside—we cannot get in. We cannot know if his wife, as she climbs the stairs, loves or hates or is entirely indifferent to this man. We cannot know what she thinks she is about to hear. We cannot know what her version of the narrative of their marriage is. We know an assortment of things about her that may make her sound unlikable. How we feel about her may be based on our own views of the contract of marriage—whether in the past we have ever been the leaver or the left. But what, at one time, were this woman's dreams? How did she feel about this man on the night he proposed to her, on the days their children were born, on this night as she climbs the stairs to change into something "more comfortable," which no longer means a negligee, no longer means that anything good will come her way? What does she see when she looks at herself in the mirror; what stories does she tell herself that allow her to get up and face each new day?

We will never know her story. She is relegated to a character actor on the fringes, someone whose motives and innermost secrets are not of primary interest to the audience. We do not know exactly what she is wearing, even, as she descends the stairs, sits with her husband, and hears the words "I want a divorce."

She is a person. Being a person does not make her good or bad; it makes her human. Her humanity hovers elusively above this scene—the scene that will make all of our narrator's dreams come true. She is the wicked witch of that narrative, the woman who will make a slew of trouble in the months to come, who will stir a cauldron boiling with rage that will cause many, including her own children, to suffer. Still, we strain to know what is in her head, in her heart, as she hears these words of her dismissal and absorbs them—as she understands that her husband is already gone. He belongs to another woman now: a younger, childless, beautiful blond with a city apartment, someone who loves his music, someone who loves him in ways she has not.

Maybe, upon hearing her husband's words, she begs him to reconsider. Maybe she says, "Fuck you." Maybe she says, "You'll pay for this." Maybe she says nothing, shock sinking into her skin, the impact of realizing that burying her head in the sand, pretending not to know about or question his late nights, has not yielded the results she expected . . . that the storm of his infidelity has not passed over eventually, as it might have for her mother's generation of wives who held their tongues, but rather has led to lightning striking the middle of their home.

The fire blazes, all-consuming—slowly at first, then all at once.

Already, our attention is turning toward her husband as he sips a scotch into the night, waiting for a decent hour to tell his lover, "It's done." It is December 10, 1991, and within a decade, he will be dead. Do we begrudge him this last decade of his life, to do with as his heart yearns? Do we begrudge his young lover her joy, knowing as we do now, with the clarity of hindsight, how blindingly happy she and this man will be for their remaining ten years? How could we begrudge such things? We, too, believe in true love . . . or want to.

Yet do we, also, begrudge the wife her anger for the way the reins of her narrative have been seized from her, relegating her to the part of a bit player in her own life?

The sun rises; the call is made; the lovers rejoice. The wife recedes, even though, in reality, she does nothing of the kind—she remains the main character of her own life. But we cannot tell the story of what is in her heart as she watches her husband walk out the door. The curtain closes; her part is over; she gives the audience the finger and is lost to us.
Act I is over. Act II has begun.

My world had cracked clear open, so wide I was falling in, but my fall was a happy one. Suddenly, Christmas was coming, and Steve was all and truly mine. I was very aware of the age-old Mistress trope of the kept woman, sitting in some apartment and waiting for her lover to fulfill his promise to leave his marriage, year after year, as her beauty fades and eventually he tires of her and she ends up alone. I was all too aware that *every* woman believes in the beginning that she will be the exception, that her love is the Real Thing, and that in the vast majority of cases this story ends only in heartbreak. But now I was standing on the other side of that story, having dodged it like a speeding bullet that whizzed by my head. I would not have to reckon with the pain of having been wrong about Steve, because I was not wrong. I was undeniably right—about our connection, our bond, our compatibility, our love.

We were not perfect people, and in the decade that we were gifted our love would not always be a perfect fairy tale, either, but it was *real*. And in what felt like the quick swipe of a rug from underneath my feet, I went from crying on the train platform as the man I loved boarded the last train for home to a series of exhilarating firsts: meeting his sons, meeting his mother, introducing him to my parents. Now, when we strolled to work together through Central Park, I didn't wonder who might see us holding hands. We were free to be a couple in the eyes of the world, with nothing left to hide.

Although I was young, the prospect of being a stepmother didn't frighten me. Steve's sons were at a beautiful age, one where they were young enough to be open to change and transition without anger and judgments, and I had always wanted to be a mother. The very first day I spent with them, at the Stamford Museum, by the time we had finished petting all the animals, my hands were interlocked with their small and trusting ones. I vowed to myself to be worthy of this trust—to put them first, just as Steve would, and to love and cherish them as my own sons.

Steve had moved into his mother's swanky apartment on Sutton Place—she traveled a great deal and was rarely there. Finally, though, we arranged a time we could all coincide. If I thought I had blown through everything in my closet the first time I'd met Steve for a drink at Cafe Luxembourg, it was nothing compared to the day I met his formidable mother! What, after all, does one wear to meet a former Miss America, 1956?

I settled on a knee-length pencil skirt, high heels, a silk blouse, and pearls, even though I was hardly a "pearl person" by any means. Steve and I met at La Cite—a scene of our affair day decadences—for a quick fortification drink before heading to his mother's apartment, and one of the regulars at the bar, who had gotten to know us well after all the time we'd spent there, took one look at me and said with a guffaw, "Who are you, Barbara Bush?"

I immediately began to sweat, fearing that instead of an elegant *Breakfast at Tiffany's* vibe I had gone full-on matron, but Steve put his arm around me and assured me, "You look absolutely perfect."

Sharon's apartment was a thing to behold. Think lots of marble and lots of silk. She was as stunning as I'd expected, though also more gracious. We sat chatting over vodka tonics together and it all seemed so easy, so natural, that I couldn't remember what I'd been so worried about. For all her tendency to meddle, Sharon was also the longtime president of the Steve Cherry fan club—she knew how miserable he had been in his marriage and just wanted him to be happy. And unlike my own parents, who had been married forever, both of Steve's parents had been through new partners and new incarnations of themselves over the years. Though I was no Miss America or Rat Packer, I came to appreciate their less conventional worldviews and flexibility.

At the end of the visit, Sharon wrapped me into a warm embrace that at the time felt merely welcoming (only later, after Steve's death, would I come to think of her love as also a form of control). Back then, through my young eyes starry with love, I only knew that everything seemed to be going right.

As for my own parents—well, I'd never seen my mother blush over one of my boyfriends before! We met them in Florida, and my mother literally stared at Steve on our entire car ride from Palm Beach to Naples; she couldn't wait to get me alone so she could gush. My father, knowing Steve had been married when we began our involvement, was skeptical going in, but by the end of the day was equally impressed, if less blushing and gawking.

After my months of anxiety during the affair, things could not have been going more smoothly. It felt, at times, that life with Steve was simply charmed. His ability to set people at ease, to get them laughing, to listen deeply and attentively, translated across all situations. I would remember this all too well later, when Kenny spoke so kindly of Steve at his memorial service—but at this time, I felt like I was living a dream.

Not that we were without challenges, of course. Divorce is not an easy thing. Yet after a contentious yearlong battle, the divorce was finalized at last. By now, Steve and I were well past the stage of meeting the parents and had been together in the open for a year, but he hadn't lost—and never would lose—his taste for grand gestures: To celebrate the divorce finally coming through, we headed off to Aspen for a week, drinking many a champagne toast "to us."

But as much as the past year had only strengthened our bond, I was still unprepared for what happened next.

It was our third day in Aspen. We were in line for the chair lift, the air clean and thin, clear and cold, mountains' sharp shapes rising up in the sky all around us, and a nice Aussie man asked in line if he could join us.

"We prefer to ride alone," Steve said with a small shake of his head.

I was more than a little shocked by this response, given his tendency to make friends everywhere we went and how open and friendly he always was. I wanted to chide him for making the Aussie man feel awkward, but knowing the man could still hear us in the line, I held my tongue, and had forgotten about it by the time the chair lift swept us up.

Into the crystal clear, chilly air we rode, holding hands with our bulky ski gloves on.

"Ugh, my hands are so cold!" I exclaimed.

Steve said mysteriously, "Well, you'll have to take your gloves off for this."

For a moment I stared at him in confusion; then understanding sank in and, with trembling fingers, I removed my gloves.

As Steve Cherry asked me to marry him, the chair lift swayed back and forth; I was so giddy that it was impossible to sit still.

"Maryellen!" he jokingly chided me. "Do you want us to fall to our deaths before I can make an honest woman of you?"

I laughed, swaying the chair even more, as Steve placed the most gorgeous pear-shaped diamond I had ever seen on my finger. *This was my life!* I couldn't believe anyone could be so fortunate, so happy. I was crying, kissing Steve, laughing, so much that I almost forgot to blurt out, "Yes, of course, yes!"

I would have said yes, I realized, had he knelt in front of my tiny apartment way back after that first night at Cafe Luxembourg. I had, from that day on, never wanted anything in my life the way I wanted this man.

At the top of the mountain, when we disembarked, the Aussie rushed over to us, beaming. "I saw the whole thing," he said. "Congratulations!"

These were the days of champagne toasts, of calls to my parents bearing only glad tidings. These were the days dreams were made of—the days that, once lost, would later haunt me.

Saying that now, I feel a twinge of guilt. Even one day with Steve, I realize, is so much more than many people get in their entire lifetimes. We had it all in those sparkling years: our youth, our health, our love, money to spend celebrating our joy. I like to think that I understood how lucky I was, and in many ways I did. I cherished Steve; I threw myself into our good fortune with every ounce of verve and full-throttle passion I had to give.

And yet the old maxim is also true: You never understand fully what you have until it's gone.

I married Stephen Patrick Cherry at The First Presbyterian Church in Naples, Florida, on November 7, 1992. Ever since my parents had relocated to Naples, I'd driven by that little white church thinking that someday I would have my wedding there, and now here I was.

I think my mother had been planning my wedding, the wedding of her only daughter, since the day I was born. My father and I knew to let her take the reins and do her thing. She was, after all, an interior designer, so I knew the reception in the Grand Ballroom of the Ritz-Carlton would be nothing short of spectacular.

She transformed it into a haven of trees with twinkling white lights, and gorgeous tables adorned with huge arrangements of exotic white flowers. Black tie, naturally! We all had rooms in the hotel, and when my father first spotted me in my wedding dress—a strapless, white-laced thing of beauty—he wept, hugging me close. My eyes grew teary, too, as I looked at him, so strikingly handsome in his black tails, and for a brief moment I thought of the fact that my parents were growing older—that they wouldn't always be here for me. Later, of course, my father would be the one to help me navigate my grief at losing my young husband. But that was nearly nine years in the future, and on my wedding day, I saw nothing but clear skies forevermore.

My father and I held hands the entire limousine ride to the church, and as we proceeded down the aisle to the traditional wedding march. Although I'd been an independent city girl for years, there was still a poignancy to the moment when I let go of my father's hand and locked eyes with Steve—my groom, my future.

Even my brother David, who officiated our wedding, broke down in tears halfway through and finally blurted, "Steve, you may kiss my sister!" The entire church broke out in laughter as Steve and I kissed intensely, sealing the bond that had existed between us from the first.

There were no terrorists in the sky. There were no falling towers, no bodies jumping from the buildings, no Ground Zero. There was no grieving widow. All of that would come for me, but not yet. Not yet. On this day, everything felt completely right.

Steve and I turned to face our family and friends as we strolled down that aisle as husband and wife. In that moment, our lives consisted of nothing but happily ever after; our fairy tale was nothing short of real, magical, and tender.

It was our life.

CHAPTER 5
SPRING TRAINING

And then, that life with my great love—that hopeful, lovestruck, dazzling life—was over. Steve was gone. When I look back on that time, these lines keep floating into my head, as if they have been tattooed there: *I don't want to be alone. I want my boys to have a father.* There would never be another Steve for me—not ever—but what about Brett and Colton? They deserved a father. I wanted my boys to grow up with a man who could guide and inspire and love them as my dad had guided me. My dad was my North Star, and I knew they needed one too.

Sometimes, when I thought about managing everything on my own for the rest of my sons' young lives, my palms would sweat and I'd feel panic course through my whole body like an earthquake shudder. And there was this terrifying question as well: Even if I tried as hard as I could and did everything in my power to give my boys a strong foundation, *what if it wasn't enough*? Would I be able to raise kind, hardworking, thoughtful, and openhearted young men as this new version of myself—a single mom rocked off my axis, no longer the happy, exuberant woman I'd been?

I had wanted children all my life, but I had never considered tackling parenthood on my own; I'd always wanted to be part of a team, to do it in partnership. Single parenting is a Herculean task, even when embarked upon with enthusiasm and volition, and I had no blueprint for this undesired Plan B, no path through my thick veil of self-doubt.

Yet when I considered my options, most of them seemed grim. Even if it hadn't been too soon, which it was, the whole idea of "dating" sounded horrible to me—wholly unappealing, not to mention logistically impractical with two young kids at home. Besides, who could possibly compete with my charismatic, romantic man who knew all the best bars in Manhattan and wrote and sang love songs for me in my apartment while I made dinner? Not a chance.

And then I would remember Russ: smoking cigarettes in the bar on my first trip back to the city after 9/11, his familiarity, his ease with the boys during the holidays, our slightly tipsy and awkward kiss that had been better than anticipated. I never expected to feel butterflies again, but I had been taken aback by the surprise kiss near the fireplace that night—not just because I'd been so rash but because I'd felt *something*; for just a moment, kissing Russ, I'd felt like a person again, a living, breathing, embodied person—not just a body going through the motions, numb to anything but the task at hand, whether it was assisting Colton in building a block tower or helping Brett with his homework. I had to admit to myself that the fleeting kiss with Russ had made me feel *alive*.

So it was that Russ and I slipped into a routine of platonically talking on the phone. There were no romantic declarations, no mention of our botched kiss, no discussions of possibilities between us; we were just friends, pals, acting as a sounding board for the other about whatever was happening in our lives. This felt sustaining, was the support I needed to keep my days buoyant and interesting, even if Russ lived in Los Angeles and I was slowly rebuilding my life in Connecticut. He kept me tethered to Steve's family, which helped me feel connected to myself. But more, something about Russ made me feel like *me* again, instead of a sad widow who had weathered a gaping and violent loss.

On the way to school pickup or while playing with a still-sleepy Colton after he woke up from a nap, I began to anticipate Russ's call. I grew accustomed to hearing his voice and soon found myself longing to hear it.

Accordingly, the tenor of our conversations began to subtly change. Soon, I looked forward to those phone calls as if they were spa treatments. Why?

Phone flirting, which quickly became the best part of my day.

Russ, like Steve, was a terrific storyteller. Out in the world, he was an introverted man and didn't go on many dates, but when he did, I received entertaining reports in the morning: *She ordered a side salad at a steak house. I want a woman who eats!* Or, *She was nice enough, but the spark just wasn't there, you know?*

Did I ever.

Our conversations were light and fun most of the time, and the first time I laughed loudly at something Russ said I almost panicked, looking around to see who was in my house—it had been that long since I'd had a belly laugh. Sometimes a smile stuck to my face for hours after we hung up. Talking to Russ was easy and comforting; he brought a sense of lightness amidst what still felt like terribly heavy days to carry.

As vibrant and funny as our conversations were, they were not without gravity. Russ always asked about the boys, and I heard the shift in his voice when he did—the great love and concern he had for them was so strong, I could have heard it through the most unstable and crackling phone connection. He wanted to know how they were feeling, what they were into, and of course he always asked in a voice that made me understand he wanted the truth, not just the forced, polite answer the grieving give to acquaintances we happen to meet at the store who know only a small part of our stories, the ones who scrunch up their face and croon, *Oh, but how are YOU?* I knew I could be honest with Russ, even vulnerable about my feelings and wishes for the future.

I had two pressing desires during this time. First, I wanted to move to a new house that wasn't saturated with memories of Steve. (Russ got it, of course, because he missed his stepbrother too.) Second, I wanted Brett at a new school, one where he wasn't the poor kid whose father died in 9/11. I had already set up a meeting with his teacher and other faculty, where I'd explained our situation and that I didn't want it brought up at school, but I knew a clean slate was impossible in our town and I wasn't willing to banish the thought of some kind of new start for my sons.

Something needed to change, or this house full of memories of all that I had lost would be like quicksand, and we'd all sink. For Steve, for myself, but especially for my boys, I couldn't let that happen.

These were the worries that kept me wide awake—sometimes all night—in those months after Steve's death.

Was it because Russ was family that I trusted him so quickly? Was it his kindness and sense of humor that reminded me of Steve and therefore endeared him to me? Was it just that I was lonely and afraid, having had my entire life ripped out from beneath me, with no time to prepare and no road map for the aftermath? Or was this—the two of us—something else? These questions chased one another in my head on an almost constant loop, a ticker tape of thoughts about what this was and what it might be and if it was crazy to even be thinking like this in the first place.

As it turned out, Russ would soon make a decision that would change my internal dialogue—and all of our lives—forever.

May arrived, fragrant and lush—it was a glorious spring, and I did my best to appreciate it, even though I still found it difficult to enjoy any beautiful sunrise or burst of blooming flowers without a pain in my heart, missing Steve. But as the season itself was a live broadcast for new beginnings—trees filling in with lush leaves, warmer and sunnier days, flowers peeking up from the last layer of snow—I was pondering one of my own.

"I need to be in a place where not everything reminds me of Steve," I told Russ. "A place where people aren't giving me *that look* whenever I pick Brett up from school or go to the park with Colton."

"The *oh-that-poor-woman* look?"

"That's the one," I said. "I can't take it anymore, and it's not good for the boys either. We need a new place where we can make new memories."

Later that month, I put words into action and decided to make a very big move—not just to a new house but to a new town, Fairfield.

Russ's reaction was, "I'll come and help you move."

When I told the boys he was coming, they were thrilled; Colton's little face lit up, and Brett whooped and said, "Yes yes yes!"

I, too, was thrilled at the idea of seeing Russ again, especially as our conversations had pulled us closer over these last few months. The day he arrived, I awoke with the once-familiar feeling of butterflies dancing in my stomach—a feeling I welcomed back, even if I wasn't sure what to make of it yet. But it was watching the pure joy on my boys' faces when they saw Russ again that really made something in me blossom and open. I felt light filling in the cracks of my heart.

I tried not to overthink it or rationalize it too much. I simply gave myself permission to feel something other than loneliness and heartache, the way I had in Bel-Air when Russ and I had shared our first awkward kiss. I let myself try on the fact that an extremely handsome man being in my home could be exciting.

I wanted so badly to feel human again, somewhat normal, whatever that would look and feel like now, and when Russ arrived, before I had even quite realized it, that's exactly how I felt.

We did lots of packing—so much packing. Russ helped me pack wardrobe cases full of my clothes and the boys', and he wrapped glasses and dishes in bubble wrap and carefully stacked these in boxes that he clearly labeled with a Sharpie. The sound of packing tape being ripped out in long sheets played like a soundtrack in nearly every room.

One afternoon I stood in the kitchen, wrapping up some of the good crystal, and through the window I saw Russ and the boys chasing one another around the lawn in the sunshine. At one point Brett looked up at me, and I knew I hadn't seen him that happy with anyone else but his father—that I hadn't seen him so unabashedly joyful in a long time. I felt heat in my chest, a warm expansion. It took me a bit to recognize the feeling, but soon I understood what it was: hope. This change, I thought, was going to be *good*.

At night we cooked hamburgers or pasta or went out for dinner at the boys' favorite places. Russ always treated. There was a sense of ease in the house again, so tactile I felt like I could grip it in my hands like a bouquet of flowers.

At bedtime—the hour I used to dread the most, the lonely young widow's hour after the so-called single-mother witching hour—I placed Colton gently in his crib, his little cheeks flushed from all the laughter and activity and togetherness. I knew he'd be sound asleep in minutes. Brett wanted Russ to sleep in his room, so we all cozied up on a large futon and settled in to watch yet another rerun of *Madeline*.

Eventually Brett fell asleep, snoring softly. Russ and I were quite close. Our hands touched. Our fingers interlocked.

This was huge for me—instinctively, I understood it as far different from a tipsy, desperate kiss. Was it right? Should I feel guilty? What next?

Before I could spiral out, we kissed—for real, mutually. It wasn't a long kiss, but it felt inevitable.

I left Brett and Russ and went to my room.

THE ROAD TO YESTERDAY

I woke up the next morning to the smell of fresh brewed coffee. Wow! Such a little thing, but it was huge ... to feel *cared for* again. And for once I'd slept soundly, restfully—not one toss or turn.

I felt my face smiling hard, felt a rekindled hope for the future burning inside me. Maybe I didn't have to be alone. Maybe things were looking up more than I could have allowed myself to imagine.

I'm sure I blushed as I entered the kitchen still in my pj's and with my bedhead hair. I gratefully grabbed a mug of coffee and thanked Russ for his thoughtfulness. The boys weren't up yet, so the two of us sat at the long farm table, moving boxes all around us, and looked in each other's eyes.

We both felt something; it was undeniable. So when Russ reached for my hand, squeezed it hard, and asked if he could come back to visit again soon, I barely let him finish his sentence before blurting out, "You sure can!"

The boys and I said our goodbyes and for the rest of that day I felt bouncy, as if I might break into a skip at any moment. Russ and I continued talking on the phone, discussing the mundane details of the day, as well as plans for his next visit and the status of my move to my new home.

"I want to get it all settled before you visit again," I said.

Three weeks later, a sleek limo pulled into my new driveway, and I watched from the kitchen window as Russ, lanky and tall, a smile on his face, stepped out of the car and the boys ran as fast they could to greet him. As they leapt into his arms, the two of us locked eyes and winked at one another.

That long weekend was as focused on time with the kids as the first one, but this time we snuck in kisses any chance the coast was clear. Only when I was sure the kids wouldn't see, though; I didn't want to confuse Brett. After all, he only knew Russ as "Uncle Russ."

Oh, how cautious I thought I was being, the comedic inverse now being so clear to me. How volitionally I mistook the familiar for the inevitable. How absolutely Not Over Steve I was, to the extent that it actually made sense to me that I should be, less than a year after his death, dating his *stepbrother*!

What did I say about an archaic royal family, about marrying the brother of the deceased king as a matter of convention, about how insane it had all seemed to me when Sharon showed up in New York with Russ in tow and I thought to myself, *Good God, this can't be a setup, can it?*

I know. I know.

And yet so began my long-distance love affair with Russ.

One long weekend, Jana stayed with the boys and I flew to Los Angeles alone. As I rode down the escalator to baggage claim, there was Russ, his eyes bright and his smile wide. My heart tumbled around in my chest with that particular, intense energy of rebound love.

We drove home holding hands, and I was anxious to see his place, a very tasteful home in Thousand Oaks. The appeal was the outside pool, which, since it was getting dark, was illuminated by lights. Russ started a fire and then fetched a bottle of wine. We sat in two rocking chairs as we sipped our wine and got all caught up and talked about our weekend plans to visit the wine country.

My familiar thoughts returned on radio blast: *I do not want to be alone with my pain. I want a father figure for my boys.* Here was Russ before me, a man my boys already loved. It had been seven months since 9/11. Russ was forty-four and had never been married. I was now thirty-eight. I had a new home in a new town with new neighbors who didn't know my story. It felt time for fresh starts, and this my own personal spring.

It all felt so *easy*.

What followed was the definition of a whirlwind romance. It turned out that Russ knew how to woo, and he did it with flair, often sending huge bouquets of flowers or fabulous cases of wine. We took a trip to France and Italy—first class all the way. Though material things were not what mattered most to me and I had not grown up with extravagance as a role model, I see now that the way Russ showered me with gifts felt reminiscent of the Steve Cherry School of Wooing—they were stepbrothers, after all, and they both understood how to use their resources to show a woman that she was never far from their minds. Even if I was no longer the naive twenty-five-year-old girl who had once fallen under Steve's thrall, I would be lying if I claimed to be immune to the way Russ, too, immersed me in the finer things in life.

He also had clearly done his research in planning our trip—perhaps even had assistance. In Chamonix, we stayed at the grand Hotel Mont-Blanc with a spectacular view of the mountains. From there we were off to the glamorous Côte d'Azur, and then, when my senses were already glutted out with pleasure, we went to Venice and stayed right on the Grand Canal in the majestic Gritti Palace.

Our trip closed out on Lake Como, definitely a contender for the most beautiful place on Earth. The holiday was magical and romantic from start to finish, Russ pulling out all the stops; our hotels will be as forever etched in my mind as the natural beauty and history that surrounded us. We spent long, leisurely lunches sipping wine and soaking up the atmosphere, followed by afternoons making love in luxurious suites, perhaps dozing off just in time to get dressed up for late dinners.

Who wouldn't feel like they were falling in love?

I seemed to have struck gold . . . again.

There is a saying that if something seems too good to be true, it's because it is. When I look back at this period of my life, so many things stand out to me that, in those moments, were walled off in a corner of my mind that I couldn't—or wouldn't—allow myself to access. After all, when Steve had seemed too amazing to be possible, the result had been the ten greatest years of my life, and even now I have not a shadow of doubt that, had his life not been cut tragically short, we would be married still today—and happy, through all the ups and downs. When I thought of how Steve had "spoiled me for other men," I was thinking only that nobody could hold a candle to him—not, of course, that if someone seemed able to, I should distrust it, erect walls of self-protection, convince myself that something was rotten when everything seemed sweet.

Though my courtship with Russ took place this millennium, it also occurred in a wildly different cultural climate, one in which "red flags" were not part of the popular dating colloquial the way they are now. Besides, a woman still in love with her dead husband, motivated at least in part by the need to distract herself from debilitating grief and in even greater part by the traditional and deeply ingrained belief that her sons need a father and it is her job to find them one, is as red as the flags waved in a bullfighting ring, so who was I to judge? And so, if there were flags—if there was red—I looked the other way: at mountains, at the shockingly blue sea, at the beautifully appointed hotel rooms in which the fortunate and famous had slept for decades or centuries. After all, Russ was kind, thoughtful, beloved by my sons, and could give me something no other man on Earth could offer: the opportunity to remain part of Steve's extended family.

Flags? What flags?

How about that, as I write this, as I can recall the intricacies of the Grand-Hotel du Cap-Ferrat or the Villa Feltrinelli in such detail that I could describe them to a court stenographer, yet somehow I barely recall a single thread of conversation Russ and I had on that trip. "Small talk," I would call it later, when discussing with friends how difficult it was to document scenes of my life with Russ—how other than a line here and a line there, our conversations stayed light, flitting on the surface of things. Perhaps, gutted as I was, I preferred it that way at the time.

Where Steve had come to me whole—where I myself had been whole at the time—Russ and I came to each other each cracked in ways we were at a loss to repair. Like many lost souls before us, we clung to each other like a kind of Krazy Glue that might fill in each other's gaps. While I had lost the love of my life to violent madness, Russ had now lost two brothers: Steve, and also his elder brother, Tom, the golden child of Russ's family of origin.

Tom had been the president of Terry Lumber, their father's company, until he died suddenly from melanoma at the tender age of forty-two. Russ of course assumed he would take on Tom's position after his passing—after all, Russ worked there, too, and had for many years. Instead, Terry sold the company straight out from under him, so determined was he that Russ not step into Tom's shoes. I remembered all of this, if from a distance... I had been married to Steve when it all went down, living on the other end of the country from the scene of Russ's primal wound.

Russ had envied Tom, but he had loved him deeply, too, and they had been close. The shock of Terry's dismissal of Russ had in some ways, however, usurped Russ's ability to mourn his brother, Tom's death becoming inextricable in his head from his father's crushing and perpetual disapproval. I knew Terry to be an unemotional man—he had not even attended Steve's funeral, for God's sake—but it would also be accurate to say that, treasured as I was by my own father, I could not, then, even wrap my mind around what it must feel like to chase a formidably successful father's approval for my entire life only to be reminded constantly of what he perceived as my many inadequacies.

This, I now understand, is the kind of lifelong wound that, while less "dramatic," causes internal fractures entirely different from the fractures I experienced in losing Steve. Traumatic though that was—and always will be—my trauma was, in a sense, born of loving and being loved. In the face of my loss, my parents and brothers rallied around me, holding me up. In the face of Russ's losses, his father closed doors in his face. Although Russ was close to his mother, a lovely and kind woman, he'd grown up in a home where he didn't experience physical affection and rarely, if ever, heard "I love you." Terry's reserve had permeated the family's ways of interacting, and whether or not he intended malice, he'd pitted his sons against one another, then left one forever out in the cold.

I had witnessed this myself that strange day when I'd seen Russ knock on the door to his own family home because he had no key, only to be greeted by his father with a formal handshake. Russ had no models of familial intimacy and demonstrative love and tenderness, which no doubt made me and my sons—already family members by proxy—as attractive to him as his being Steve's stepbrother made him to me. We were two drowning people clutching to each other to stay afloat . . . but who thinks of such things while gorging on fine French dining and succulent wines and the highest mountains and deepest blue seas? Who thinks of such things when still in the brain fog of great loss?

Here's a phrase to live by: *If something seems too good to be true, it's because it is.*

Here's another: *Hindsight is 20/20.*

At the time I was trying to look forward, not backward, now with Russ at my side, which felt right. What I wasn't expecting, therefore, was another call in August, almost a year after 9/11, on Brett's seventh birthday.

We were at Sharon's in Los Angeles when Laura, a neighbor of mine in Connecticut, called. "The police are here," she said, her voice frantic and tearful. "They want to talk to you."

I felt my stomach drop; what now? What new disaster was this?

As Russ and Sharon continued making birthday preparations for Brett, I stepped outside, feeling weak in the knees.

The police told me that part of Steve's body had been identified—part of his femur bone. I swallowed hard, trying to take in this information. I imagined the people who were spending hours and hours in the morgue, trying to identify to whom this or that bone belonged. A snapshot of hell. The police let me know that I had forty-eight hours to identify the remains.

I hung up, went inside, and asked Russ if we could go for a walk.

I didn't know what to do, and the two of us discussed this utterly surreal development carefully as we padded slowly along. What would be the upside of seeing a small piece of bone in a box? Seeing Steve's work ID had been jarring enough, but at least it was still intact and showed his face.

We had mourned Steve. He was gone. We agreed that to have another memorial—which would certainly re-traumatize all of us—was a terrible idea and would offer no comfort to those of us who were still living and grieving. We were trying to start a new life; we were not trying to forget Steve in the process—that would never happen—but we certainly didn't need to revisit the violence. I could not imagine telling the boys that we were going to pick up a part of their father's body. What could a bone tell us that our hearts could not?

Nothing, we decided. Nothing at all. But it was another grim reminder, yet another shock to the heart and the system after eleven months of almost relentless and disorienting shock waves.

I wanted—and needed—to move forward.

THE ROAD TO YESTERDAY

For Thanksgiving 2002, Russ and I traveled to visit a couple I'd been close to in Fairfield, who had now moved to Texas. We were all feeling festive, the tyranny of those "first holidays" without Steve finally lifted from my head.

On Thanksgiving morning, the turkey already baking in the oven, yummy and homey smells permeated the house. Downstairs, I heard the pop of a champagne bottle, and as I descended the stairs from the guest room, I saw mimosas being served in the kitchen. Surveying the scene for a moment at a distance, I felt like I was watching a movie about somebody else's beautiful life—like I was standing outside my body and watching, as a very fortunate woman named Maryellen made her voice excited and friendly as she, too, entered the kitchen and accepted a mimosa.

Just as quickly as the sense of separation had come, it was gone, and there I was in a newly appointed kitchen, in the home of my close friends, drinking champagne while my sons happily chowed on breakfast. This was *my* life. It would never be a life of innocence again, after losing Steve, but it could be a beautiful life nonetheless. Maybe, I dared to think, it could even be sweeter for my having known such pain—now, I would appreciate the good times even more deeply.

Abruptly, Russ grabbed my hand. I noticed that he appeared halting and nervous, but sometimes being around people he didn't know well brought that out in him, so I didn't think much of it.

Holding my hand tightly, Russ led me outside. As we took a seat by the pool, for a moment I worried that his apparent anxiety might mean something had gone wrong—but before I knew it, he had withdrawn a small velvet box from his pocket and revealed a (very large!) emerald-cut diamond.

Like a schoolgirl, I gasped at the sight.

"Will you be my wife?" he asked simply. He never had been a man of many words, but these five sure caught my attention.

Once I had exclaimed "Yes!" and our friends saw us hugging, they dashed out to join us outdoors. Russ had spilled the beans to them that morning (ahh, hence the champagne) and they were thrilled for us. How fated it all must have seemed to them, I realize—what kismet!

Is that what everyone believed? If not, no one told me otherwise.

We headed inside to find Brett and Colton, off playing now, to share the big news. I will never forget the sight of Russ propping one boy on each knee as he told them we were going to marry, or the pure joy on Brett's gleaming face as he wrapped his little hands around Russ's neck and asked, "Can I call you Dad now?"

In that moment, I did not think of Steve. I did not feel any pangs at the thought of his being usurped in his title of "Dad," or for his sons' affection. I knew Steve, and I knew he would never want his sons fatherless, lonely, aching for him. The soaring happiness I felt was, I knew deep in my bones, a happiness Steve would want for me—for all of us.

It wasn't until the flight back to Connecticut, alone with the boys as Russ headed back to California, that I felt my first stirrings of discomfort. With both boys fast asleep, I sat staring at my new engagement ring and what it represented. I was going to remarry. I wouldn't be alone after all. Everything was better—everything was good.

And yet I felt uneasy every time I looked down at my extravagant ring. It was . . . so big. I was surprised by how uncomfortable it made me—after all, I was no stranger to luxury thanks to both Steve and Russ. Yet I felt uncomfortable flashing this ring around out in the ordinary world; it seemed a ring made for the Côte d'Azur or a palace in Venice, not for my everyday life as a stay-at-home mom. I loved living it up, sure, but at home, my boys and I led fairly average, if comfortable, lives. This ring felt, though it pained me to think it, ostentatious and *not me*.

Only a few weeks later, out to lunch with Sharon to celebrate the engagement, I tentatively mentioned to her that I thought my ring was a bit too pretentious for my lifestyle. Her comeback: "Oh, my dear, there is no such thing as a diamond too big for a woman." Of course, I would later learn that Sharon had picked my ring out with Russ, had guided his hand, just as Russ had obtained assistance in planning our whirlwind trip to France and Italy. While Steve had never been averse to a little flash, everything he had ever done to woo me had felt completely authentic to him—his personality, his tastes, his haunts and passions, and especially his knowledge of me.

Russ, by contrast, seemed to be courting me by committee. Did my soon-to-be husband really know me? Did I know him?

But the drowning do not pause to ask such questions. On and on, we clung.

After a short engagement—perfect for those who don't wish to overthink things—I married my second husband, Russell Bishop Mullin, on the beach in Honolulu.

Three days before the intimate affair, Russ, Brett, Colton, and I came down with a horrible stomach bug. The night before, we were convinced that we would have to cancel since we were spending most of the late evening with Colton in the ER. Yet the next morning, everyone was miraculously entirely better, and the show went on.

Even all these years later, I sometimes wonder what might have happened if we had temporarily called it off.

While Steve's and my wedding had been elaborate, this gathering was intimate, with only Sharon; Terry; Steve's brother Shawn and his husband, Vincent; Brett; Colton; Russ; and me. I wore a simple white wraparound skirt with a white camisole and—my favorite part of my attire—a traditional Hawaiian floral headpiece, a haku lei, in my hair. As we said our vows, any petty doubts I'd had about my too-big ring (*oh, what a terrible problem!*) or rebuilding a new relationship with Sharon (*I wanted to remain part of Steve's family, remember?*) drifted off with the tide, and as we toasted to Russ's and my many years of happiness, I felt peace settling over me.

After living as a widow for a little over a year, I was now Maryellen Mullin. I had found a steady, loving partner who loved me and adored my boys. It had happened so quickly and naturally (in some ways, at least) that it was no stretch for me to believe that it was literally meant to be. Once again, I was part of a team. My interior script had flipped: *You will not be alone.*

How wrong I turned out to be.

CHAPTER 6
THE MARRIAGE PLOT

Imagine the opening scene of a film. Montages of a wedding, small and intimate, the bride sporting a lovely flower headpiece; the happy couple driving away; a small plane taking off for Kauai. Pan in on the luxurious Princeville hotel, slowly move closer to show a woman—the bride from the montage. Up close we see she's thirty-eight, not the young and blushing bride of predictable fairy tales. She stands on her hotel room balcony, overlooking the island splendor. From below, noises of good-time vacationers drift up from the pool.

The bride is dressed in her sexy swimsuit—she's still got it!—with a sarong tied at her hips. Her excitement is palpable in the way she holds her body. She turns to where her new husband sits lounging in a patio chair. These days, he would be playing with his iPhone, but as this film takes place in the opening days of 2003, we'll give him a newspaper, from the days when Serious Men still read Serious Papers.

The man is handsome but remote, not looking at his bride, focused entirely on whatever he is reading.

"Hey!" his wife says flirtatiously, ruffling his hair. "Let's go down to the pool and have a cocktail and some lunch. Maybe, if you're good, I'll let you rub sunscreen on my back."

The man barely looks up—maybe he does not look up at all. Maybe he absentmindedly straightens his hair where she's mussed it. "I'm happy here," he mutters, turning a page in his paper. "More privacy."

At this comment, the woman looks down at him expectantly—privacy, yes, that is what honeymoons are for, after all! She stands, waiting for her groom to take her in his arms and ravage her there on their "more private" balcony—sure, that beats lunch and a cocktail, yes, please. But a few beats go by—how long will our director leave her hanging as her anticipation turns to awkwardness, as the audience begins to understand that the man has no such thing in mind, that he has, perhaps, already forgotten she is even standing there? Thirty seconds? Longer?

Finally (the script would read "with false cheer" before her lines), the woman says, "Okay, no problem, honey. I'm going to go on down and get some sun. You sure you don't want to join me?"

Several more beats of silence before the man, still not looking up, says, "I'm good."

We watch the woman leave the swanky hotel room alone with her beach bag over her shoulder, sunhat on, the door clicking shut behind her. The man does not look after her.

In the hallway, the woman takes several deep breaths, then squares her shoulders and heads down to the pool alone.

What, in the movie version of this couple's life, are the chances they would not be divorced by the time the credits roll?

But, of course, real life is craftier than film. Real life will deal you hands for which you were never prepared. Real life will make the sad ending of a movie about love's disillusionment look like child's play. And so, things don't end that way. Stella doesn't get her groove back; no one shows up holding a radio above his head blasting the woman's favorite song. Down below, out of her husband's line of sight (not that he's looking), the new bride demurely arranges her towel on a lounge chair, sits, and pulls a book from her bag. This is the first day of her honeymoon, for Chrissakes. She is not supposed to be sitting here alone, reading a book.

This is the marriage that will teach her that "supposed to be" is not a thing she can touch, not a thing she can prove even exists, except in her memories.

Brett, Colton, and I had only just moved to Fairfield, but here we were, packing house again, our "new beginning" barely off the ground. I told myself that change was good—that my sons would have a far fresher start in California than they could get by just moving to a new town in Connecticut. In California, nobody would know about our pasts unless we chose to share the information. Although September 11, 2001, still hung heavy in the air in towns and suburbs full of those who commuted to Manhattan for work, elsewhere in the country, Americans were getting on with their lives.

Leaving the East Coast felt both wrong and right, a confusing muddle, and so I did what I was doing a lot of back then: turned my mind off and instead of analyzing, simply *acted*. By February, my sons and I had moved across the country into Russ's bachelor pad.

Although I was happy (if sometimes a bit ambivalent about my mother-in-law) to be back in the fold of Steve's family with my boys, in California I also found myself profoundly lacking in the kind of support network I'd taken for granted for most of my life. My longtime besties, Gina and Anne, were now thousands of miles away. I thought of how frustrated and frantic Gina and I had been when she'd been stuck in New Jersey and couldn't make it to my house immediately when the Twin Towers fell; now, she would have to book a plane ticket, get to the airport, go through security, wait at her gate, fly for six hours, land, claim her luggage, and get to my new home if we needed each other. My brothers, my parents, were all equally far away. Russ worked all day and Brett was at school. My adorable Colton was fabulous company, but I craved adult companionship.

Although I was not much of a practicing Catholic anymore, I'd been raised in the church and had always experienced community and fellowship there. Maybe the same could hold true now. But when I asked Russ if we could go to the lovely Catholic church near his—our—home, he dismissed the idea. "I'm not religious," he told me—end of discussion.

Already, I was beginning to figure out that community was not the priority for Russ that it was for me, and that if I wanted to find one, I was on my own. And so, one Sunday, I dressed the boys in their Sunday best, took extra care with my hair and makeup to make a good impression on our new neighbors, and off we went to Mass.

Upon arrival, the younger children were rounded up by cheerful Sunday school teachers and corralled, leaving me unaccompanied in the pew throughout the service. I felt uncomfortable at first, but soon the reassuring ritual of Catholic Mass made me feel at home. Here, at last, was something familiar! I knew the words of all the prayers, the recitations, when to kneel and when to stand. Though some of the hymns were different from those of the church of my youth, I took comfort in the fact that all over the world, any wandering Catholic could stumble into any Sunday Mass and find themselves at home. Lulled by the incense and the sense of the sacred, I also felt closer to Steve, as though he might be right beside me, on the other side of a thin veil through which I could not see.

I left Mass in a lighter mood, despite having met no one, and went to queue up to claim my boys.

It was there that I met Cindy Henderson, who would ultimately become one of my closest friends in my new neighborhood. She, too, was waiting to claim her son; she, too, had just moved to the area. We began chatting animatedly in the way of women who have been starved for female comradery, with an instant intimacy and excitement.

"We're having a block party today!" she told me. "You must come! Bring your husband. I'll introduce you to everyone."

Although I had traveled to many beautiful and exciting locations around the world, it would be impossible to overstate how over-the-moon excited I was to receive an invitation to a block party—I immediately raced home to tell Russ.

He was napping when the boys and I returned, but I woke him, too giddy to contain myself, and told him, "We're going to a party!"

Russ seemed disoriented, annoyed. I began regaling him with the meet-cute story of my new friendship, telling him how happy I was to have met a fun, cool mom friend and how she'd promised to introduce us around.

"I don't feel like making small talk," Russ said, not unkindly. Still, I felt myself deflating before his eyes, the air leaking out of my bright red balloon.

"But, honey," I urged, "I don't know anyone around here, and it would be good for me and the boys to meet people in our new home."

Russ just shrugged. "You go, then," he said. "It's my day off. I won't know anybody there."

By this point, my anger had ignited, though I tried to press it down. "Russ," I said more firmly, "the boys and I have moved all the way across the country for you, and you won't even go to a block party a few blocks away for us?"

"This is ridiculous," Russ said. "Don't be a drama queen."

With tears in my eyes, I left the room.

Was I being a drama queen? It was "just" a block party, after all—a last-minute invitation. But then I imagined our roles reversed: Russ dashing into our home, full of excitement, asking me to go somewhere he desperately wanted to go, and me refusing him for no particular reason. I could not even fathom doing that. I admit that I also thought of Steve doing this—tried to picture him dismissing my happiness or desires so that he could lie around on the couch all day—and it was equally unfathomable.

Though resentment and confusion simmered in me, I got the boys changed into play clothes and put on a more casual outfit, and off we went to the block party alone.

My heart hammered anxiously in my chest as we approached the crowd of strangers, but almost immediately Cindy spotted me and dashed over, saying how happy she was that we'd made it and offering me a drink.

"Where's your husband?" she asked, and for the first but nowhere near the last time, I fibbed that Russ wasn't "feeling well" and that he sent his regrets. Given that he hadn't been at church with me either, my story felt credible, but already I was worrying about what I would say the next time Russ refused to accompany me somewhere. How many "sick days" could my new husband have?

Soon, though, my anxieties melted away as my boys ran around with the other kids and I talked, ate, and drank with my new neighbors. The atmosphere was welcoming, familiar—I knew that I could become friends with many of these people, and my heart rested easier.

As the sun set and everyone let their hair down even more, some people dancing as a DJ spun pop music peppered with 1980s tunes and even some Frank Sinatra here and there, Cindy grabbed my hand and said, "You *have* to go get your husband and bring him! We all want to meet him!"

By now, my anger and trepidation had loosened a bit from red plastic cups of wine that reminded me of parties in college, and I impulsively agreed. My new friends promised to keep an eye on Brett and Colton, and off I went to round up Russ. At the very least, I knew he couldn't possibly *still* be asleep.

I found him sitting in his favorite rocking chair with a beer in hand. This, I was already realizing, was how Russ spent most of his time when he wasn't at work. My stomach churned with that feeling of walking on eggshells around a man, afraid of triggering his ire, afraid of making my desires nakedly known only to find out that he just . . . didn't care.

Still, I persisted. "Please," I begged him, when he at first refused all over again. "This means so much to me. If you love me, you will come with me. It's not that much to ask."

Russ rose from his chair. "Fine," he said. "If my going to some inane block party on a block that isn't even ours is what will prove my love to you, sure, let's roll." But he wasn't making a joke—I could see that he was irritated. And as he drove us back to the party, he grew angry. "I can't believe you're making me do this! Fine, I'm going to the *big important party*—are you happy now?"

Tears filled my eyes, and I regretted intensely having gone back for Russ at all. Was he going to humiliate me now in front of all my new friends? Would he punish me for making him come? I almost begged him to turn the car around, but of course Brett and Colton were still at the party.

However, no sooner did we arrive back at the party than Russ's demeanor changed entirely. Here, again, was the affable, kind man who had supported and courted me after Steve's death. I saw him shaking hands with the other men with warmth and a smile, attentively asking questions of the women, going off to roughhouse with the boys until they squealed, and I began to feel a little bit crazy. Who had I been talking to, back at our house? It wasn't the Russ I'd fallen in at least a kind of love with—the Russ I'd moved across the country to join my life with.

I began to understand, then, that Russ had a public self and a private self, and the work of putting on his public face was often exhausting to him—he preferred his rocking chair, his beer, his solitude. He would not humiliate me, it turned out, and on the way home later he even admitted that he'd had "a good time" and that he'd met "a lot of nice people," but never once did he reference his vitriolic resistance to attending or apologize for the way he'd acted toward me. It was just as if those words had never been exchanged.

I instinctively understood that if I wanted to keep the peace, I would pretend the same.

In the movie version of my marriage with Russ, you might see another montage right about here: one of Russ sitting in that damn rocking chair night after night, drinking beer after beer, a skilled makeup artist indicating time passing by adding gray to his hair or new lines on his face. In film, we can fast-forward something, present it in a way such that the audience knows this is how the years passed. But in life, we have no fast-forward button. We are stuck in our days, in our hours, in our minutes, as they tick by. And in those slow early months, I began to accept the truth of what happens when you marry a man you have known only on brief vacations, in the grip of your own grief and fear of loneliness.

Though I had—even if it was hard to admit to myself—married Russ largely because of his connection to Steve, I gradually began to understand that this marriage was going to be the antithesis of my first, and that it was up to me to somehow adjust to that reality and make the best of it, lest I upend my sons' lives all over again.

As a stay-at-home mother living in a new state, the highlight of my day was Russ coming home. My new husband. Yet I quickly noticed a pattern of how our nights would go. Russ would grab a Heineken, go sit outside in "his" rocking chair by the fireplace, and listen to Bob Dylan or some other music that felt brooding and depressing to me. Oh, and of course he'd light up a Marlboro cigarette. Those damn cigarettes! They became, in a way, the metaphorical embodiment of how something can seem one way when you're dating and long distance, and an entirely different way when you're living with it every single day.

While Russ and I had enjoyed a passionate sex life during our long-distance dating, making urgent love and then lying around decadently smoking cigarettes in bed, which made me feel like a glamorous femme fatale from an old movie, once we were living together, his cigarettes remained but our sexual life all but evaporated into thin air. I could not have known this when we saw each other only every few weeks or months, but I soon learned that Russ's sex drive was significantly lower than mine, and if he gave any thought to how often newlyweds "should" make love, then his conclusions were disappointing.

Most likely, though, he never gave it any thought at all.

I always knew when he wanted sex because only then would he initiate affection—holding my hand or patting my ass or kissing me. The rest of the time, he almost never touched me at all. I continued to initiate affection, however—first because I craved it and later because I wanted my boys to see me and their beloved "Dad" exemplifying a happy relationship. (As it turns out, of course, you can't hide anything from kids. Brett would later remark to me that Russ and I seemed "like roommates." Though of course he was too young to articulate it at first, he eventually said, "You two don't make sense together as a married couple." Alas, it was not for lack of trying!)

The truth of real life is far more complicated than movie-truth. This is the truth I would now have to learn to live with: that Russ was one of the kindest, softest-spoken human beings I'd ever known, and he wanted desperately to be a good father and husband, yet despite what he believed he wanted—a family—he was ultimately an incorrigible loner. He'd been a bachelor for forty-four years for a reason. I believed he loved me, and I *knew* he loved his new sons, and yet the immovable fact was, Russ had lived alone his entire adult life because he *liked* his lifestyle just the way it was. And if I was to be his wife, I would have to accommodate his preferences, not the other way around.

Several months into living together in California in the house Russ had long owned, we mutually decided that his bachelor home wasn't big enough for a young family. We wanted more room for the boys to run around.

In this one way, Russ and I were always united: We both wanted the absolute best life we could offer our sons. We considered all our options and eventually determined that we would build a house together in the town of Calabasas.

For me, this was a godsend in my already-flatlining marriage. I went into full-scale planning mode, as—like my mother—I've always adored design and decorating. Russ and I split duties: He would design the exterior of the house and I the interior. We were a good team in this endeavor, in working together to make a wonderful home in which to raise our family. Building our own dream home as a pair brought us closer, even if not romantically, and served as a salve for the aching part of my heart that feared I'd made a terrible mistake by rushing into this marriage.

Romantic love is a complex thing. On the one hand, many see it as transient, an impractical foundation on which to build a life, as it is commonly understood to be fleeting, impermanent. I knew from my decade with Steve that this wasn't true—sure, after ten years I'd no longer experienced the sensation of my stomach falling down an elevator shaft every time my husband walked into a room, but my love for Steve had never stopped feeling deeply romantic, and our attraction, if less frantic than in the early years, had never stopped feeling intense and mutual. I often thought of the stunning night of passion we had shared in front of the fire just before Steve's death. This was proof, I knew, that the kind of love those in blasé marriages tell themselves is only "make-believe" *is* real, if rare. Yet also, I frequently scolded myself for my expectations being too high. I'd had a decade with Steve that was better than what many people ever feel for even a week of their lives. I chided myself for being "greedy," for expecting Russ—an entirely different person—to somehow replicate his stepbrother.

And so it goes. I, like many women—and men, of course, too—learned to live without romantic fulfillment. I derived my joy from settling into a "normal" life again with my sons: T-ball and soccer games and Cub Scouts, a school they loved with great new friends, a world far from the shadow of tragedy that had trailed behind us in Connecticut. And whatever Russ lacked as a husband, I told myself he made up for in spades as a father. Whenever the boys didn't have scheduled sports events on the weekends, Russ, Brett, and Colton could be found at Denny's for breakfast before heading off to the driving range. Russ had promised to love my sons as his own, and never did he renege on that promise—to this day, their breakfasts at Denny's with their dad remain some of their favorite memories. And although Russ didn't much care for meeting new people and didn't maintain many friendships, he did have a long-standing best friend, Dan Ziggers, and every single Tuesday we went to the Ziggerses' home for Taco Tuesdays. We also went to Mexico annually with them, such that our children felt more like cousins than friends.

A woman learns to adjust. I was married to a successful man who loved my sons madly. Many women would kill for such a life, I reminded myself. It was only because I'd been so exceptionally lucky with Steve—because I'd known the kind of Big Love that many believe exists only in movies and love songs—that I didn't understand that this was what most marriages were like . . .

In 2004, Russ and I bought a second home in Victor, Idaho. It was an off-the-beaten-path location of which few people had heard, but a realtor who spent the day taking us to view unaffordable homes in Jackson Hole had given us the inside scoop that by just driving over the pass that connects Wyoming and Idaho, we could find a spectacular home in our price range.

What excellent advice this turned out to be. Russ and I drove into a small golf community named Teton Springs, and the moment we met our new realtor, Bonny, I knew we were in the right place (and had the inkling that Bonny and I would also become lifelong friends).

Soon, our entire family fell absolutely in love with the then-obscure Victor, Idaho. At Teton Springs, Russ and our boys could indulge their golf passion to their hearts' content; the area was picturesque, with stunning mountain views; and the people were all far more down-to-earth and friendly than those in more illustrious and coveted communities. Our plan was to spend summers and all school holidays there.

Though I'd never even heard of Teton Springs or set foot in Idaho previously, I sensed something magic about the place and couldn't shake the idea that somehow Steve had led me here for a reason. Inside, I chided myself for such superstitious thinking and attributed it to my inability to get over Steve because of my quiet dissatisfaction with my new marriage.

Soon, though, it was my skepticism I began to doubt.

Within the first few weeks of our being at Teton Springs, our former realtor/now friend, Bonny, called and said that our neighbors across the street wanted to have us all over. Miraculously, Russ put up no complaint.

Well, it turned out that one of those neighbors, Penny, had worked close to the World Trade Center and felt quite traumatized by 9/11, so she and her husband had moved to Victor in the hopes of finding a safe and quiet place to raise their daughter. Penny and I immediately bonded, and knowing that someone in my new circle understood what I was carrying inside, I felt instantly at home in my new community.

It was what happened next, however, that blew my mind entirely: One night in July 2004, Russ and I were at a neighborhood party, and Penny and her husband had invited a man named Grant Wood. While they were chatting with Grant, telling him about some of the new people he'd be meeting—in other words, us!—Penny said of me, "The poor gal lost her husband on 9/11 and has two young boys." Grant responded, "I lost a dear friend that day as well, Steve Cherry." Needless to say, Penny nearly fell over. "Well, Grant," she said, stunned, "you're about to meet your friend's widow."

To my utter shock, it turned out that Grant was also dear friends with my popular-if-formidable mother-in-law and had known Steve since childhood. When Penny introduced us and our eyes locked, we hugged tightly and shared a few tears over Steve and the incredible coincidence. That summer, Grant regaled Brett and Colton with endless stories about their dad from before either Russ or I had known him—a gift I will treasure forever.

There was another gentleman at the party that night, too, who ended up playing an even more significant role in my life, though of course I had no knowledge of it then. I only knew that when Penny introduced us to Michael Donovan and he whipped around to say hello, I noticed his kind eyes and warm smile instantly, in a way I had been struck only once before in my life: the lunch at Palio where I briefly met Steve for the first time. I also found his crisp, long-sleeved pink-and-white-striped shirt charming—I love a man in a pink shirt.

By the night's end, all the men had scheduled a tee time together for the next morning, and the women had made a plan to hang out at the Teton Springs pool with the kids. After moving from town to town, state to state, it looked as though I had finally found the community I'd been longing for.

Hence began the summer of 2004. Each night was dinner at someone else's home, a gaggle of talking and eating and drinking and merriment. With new friends to hang out with daily, my sons were thriving. Russ traveled back and forth to Victor every other weekend because he of course had to work, but although I missed him—or at least missed the idea of him and what I wished we were together—I was never too lonely because I had so many new friends with whom to dally away pleasurable hours.

For the first time since September 11, 2001, something stilled and relaxed inside me. I would always carry grief for Steve, of course, but I no longer experienced the pain daily, and I felt grateful for any moment I was able to forget. Here in my new life, surrounded by friends and an embracing community—including people like Penny and Grant, who understood my pain—rather than striving for numbness or distraction, I began to genuinely heal. I told myself that now that I was recovering and no longer comparing everything to my life with Steve, perhaps my second marriage would be able to blossom too.

There are many kinds of pain in the world, some obliterating and world-shattering and others quiet, private. One of the quietest and yet most devastating is the pain of trying to *make* somebody else love you the way you need to be loved, as there is no outcome for this, really, but failure and shame.

Every Friday, when Russ came back to Victor from California, I tried over and over again, like a lab rat that simply cannot learn the maze that is its home, to produce a "perfect homecoming" that he would recognize. I'd don a flirty summer dress, light the candles, have his favorite beer chilling on ice. Sometimes it was cheese and crackers out on a platter, a glass of wine already poured when he came in. All I craved was a simple, "Oh, you look so beautiful," or even, "Damn, it's good to be home," but Russ, ever the stoic, did not know how to give me what I needed—so my efforts went unacknowledged, unspoken, and my shame and resentment grew. Was Russ purposely withholding kind words from me, to keep me in some loop of insecurity? While it sometimes seemed that way to me at the time, I realize now that of course that was not the case.

When Colton greeted Russ with signs proclaiming, welcome home, daddy! he, too, went largely ignored as Russ cracked a beer and lit a cigarette—and I know the boys meant more to Russ than anything in the world. But I'd ignored the warning signs—the warmth, affection, and approval Russ's father perpetually withheld from him; the ways in which Russ simply did not understand what it meant to be part of a loving family. And when you are a man, nothing in this country's culture tells you that perhaps you might need to change or grow—you are encouraged to believe that others should simply accommodate themselves to suit you. After all, wasn't that precisely what I had done? Left my still-new home in Fairfield, my family, my friends, my son's school, all behind to mold my life to Russ's? Wasn't our very presence here—waiting for him, dressed up with signs and cheese platters and drinks on ice—*proof* that whatever Russ was doing was working out for him just fine? What incentive could he possibly have to change?

    I began to fear that even if, somehow, he came to a place of *wanting* to, he would not even know where to begin.

CHAPTER 7
DREAM A LITTLE DREAM

And so, time passed. Two years had gone by since that first summer of healing in Victor in 2004, and suddenly, it was the disconcerting summer of 2006. Despite all my well-intended promises to myself to be the most chill and undemanding of wives, to make the best of my privileged circumstances, to stop wanting for more, it is, at the bottom line of it all, hard to live in a cold marriage. Or (even now I feel the need to backpedal, to caveat), *it was hard for me*.

After three years of marriage, I began having trouble staying calm amidst my own internal storms of doubt and frustration, and the more storm clouds gathered, the more resentful I became of both Russ and myself. On the surface, of course, everything seemed to be going smoothly. My boys were thriving, and from any outsider's perspective, Russ and I were happily married and living in a beautiful home in a spectacular part of the world. We had friends and resources, laughter, and comfort. Why, then, did I feel, more each day, like I was captaining a ship without knowing the destination or even how to read the map?

Russ and I had such different relational styles, such different family backstories, and we couldn't seem to arrive in a place where his emotional distance and my needs for playfulness and passion could connect. And then there is also the deep and internalized shame of living a lie, of portraying your life to all but a few closest confidantes in a false light, for although we appeared a happy family, behind the scenes Russ and I were more like roommates—and even in that sense, only *occasional* roommates, as he continued to spend workweeks in California.

I was careful never to discuss my private life with most of Russ's and my mutual friends, not wanting to disrespect him or for word of our issues to get out, but I had confided in old friends like Gina and Anne that I didn't know what more I could do to draw him into the emotional intimacy I longed for and that had felt so real during our courtship. Was it all in my mind? Was I being ungrateful? Was I not trying hard enough, or was I trying in the wrong ways?

"Mare," Anne said to me on the phone one night when Russ was not in town, "we were all so devasted for you after Steve's death. You and the boys had lost so much. It seemed like such a miraculous thing, for you and Russ to end up together. But when I look back, I'm sorry I didn't advise you to wait, to make sure it was right. It was all just so horrible—what happened to Steve—we were all reeling. No one was thinking straight."

I knew Anne would never judge me, that she loved me unconditionally, and yet as the truth of her words settled over me, I judged myself. I'd seen and felt what I wanted—needed—to see and feel, projecting onto Russ my ideas of what marriage was and believing we saw the same picture of our future in our minds. Now forty-two, I alternately wanted to take that newly widowed thirty-seven-year-old version of myself in my arms and hold her, and to shake her and tell her, *Your husband just died! What are you even doing, falling into the arms of his stepbrother?*

My all-consuming fears of being alone with my pain had led me to behave rashly; I had no doubt misrepresented myself to Russ as badly as he had misrepresented himself to me. We had never discussed any of the things a couple should discuss before becoming engaged, never agreed on what we each needed out of a marriage. Instead, I'd gone from sucking down postcoital cigarettes to moving my sons to the other side of the country. I'd contorted myself into whatever I needed to be to make it work.

Though I'd attended therapy and grief groups after Steve's death, I now realized I'd spent scant little of that time looking at my horror of being alone and where it came from, considering why I felt, despite a supportive community, close-knit family, deep friendships, and financial security, that I could not survive as a single mother. I was not some June Cleaver throwback—I'd worked at Morgan Stanley for a decade, living on my own in Manhattan, for God's sake! Why had I allowed myself to settle for a man I barely knew, confused familial ties for true intimacy, accepted that my husband's stepmother had been responsible for many of the finer details of our courtship?

If at times I blamed Russ for ignoring me (and his father for ignoring him), mainly I blamed myself. I felt guilty when I grew frustrated with the distance between us, and I felt guilty for comparing him to Steve. Loving the man I would always miss, while at the same time so desperately wanting to be in love with my *living* husband—and feeling unseen by him—was like a tornado in my heart that lifted every day, then died down, then lifted again.

I wanted peace, not a daily storm. I was restless, tired of being inside my own brain.

By the summer of 2006, I had been seeing a marriage counselor on my own for two years (because Russ had no interest in going with me) and was reaching the end of my rope. How could I solve our joint marital problems on my own? On my own, the only possible solution was, *Stop wanting more*. I had tried that for three years, yet my discontent only grew. Why was I the only one fighting for us? Why was I the only one on this ship?

During that time, Michael Donovan had slowly become my dearest and closest on-the-ground friend. Around him, I did not feel the constant need to tamp myself down. I could be emotional, messy, determined, and goofy with him.

The summer I'd met Michael—our first summer in Victor—we'd spent a lot of time at the pool, and then invariably we both ended up at the same friends' house for dinner. Michael's daughter, Julia, was the same age as my boys. While earlier in our marriage my life had seemed to stop in its tracks when Russ was away all week for work, increasingly I didn't feel lonely and adrift anymore when he was gone. I had a whole new boisterous crew, and in that group I had Michael, who was easy to talk to about anything and everything.

I teased him about being the "perfect catch" and told him I'd be on the lookout for that perfect woman for him. His response was a jovial, but honest, "Hell no!" He'd been married twice, he said, and had no intention of walking down the aisle a third time.

I can relate, I thought. If I could have been my thirty-seven-year-old self again, the thing I would have feared most would not have been being single but rather being alone inside a marriage.

Then I would see Russ with my sons—witness their tight and beautiful bond—and chastise myself anew. I had done what I sought and found them a loving father. *My own feelings don't matter*, I told myself again and again. *My sons are more important.*

Still, the storm continued to brew.

We all lie to ourselves at times, and at this, I realized, I was becoming an expert. For, even as I was going to marital counseling to learn to accept things as they were, what lie could smooth over the fact that, increasingly, I looked forward to seeing Michael more than I did my own husband? That I felt less actively unhappy when Russ and I were apart, because then I couldn't crave a kind of attention or reaction from my husband that was not going to be forthcoming? That I had started to think entirely too often about the way Michael's deep blue eyes always seemed to contain a sparkle that set him apart from others around us and drew my gaze to him?

Although I tried to deny it and fought as hard as I could, at some point I had to stop lying to myself. My feelings for Michael began to preoccupy me, and I was no longer a girl: I understood that this was not how one was supposed to feel about a platonic friend.

To make matters worse—because it would have been far easier if my feelings were unrequited and merely a harmless fantasy—I noticed that Michael's feelings for me were also becoming clear. In our close-knit group of friends, it was not uncommon for men and women to pal around together harmlessly—but as our friendship grew closer, Michael showed less and less interest in even casually dating other women. I saw the way the sparkle in his eyes ignited when I walked into a room. I knew that the things he confided in me about his first two marriages were not things he casually discussed with the whole group. And as our intimacy grew, I found myself likewise confiding in him about my floundering unhappiness with Russ, who had done "nothing wrong," I kept stressing, yet could not seem to make me feel alive and deeply known in the ways my first husband had.

At first, it had been easy to tell myself that no man could compare to Steve and that my expectations for Russ were merely unrealistic. But as my friendship with Michael blossomed, although Steve Cherry remained as magical in my memory as ever, I began to realize that my eternal love for him was not stopping me from keenly feeling the magic Michael also possessed, a magic of his own that made me feel wildly awake and attuned, increasingly craving the next time I would see him.

Forbidden love was a road I had been down before, but now *I* was the married one. I knew I could not cheat on Russ, or I would never forgive myself. That could not be his repayment for having embraced my sons and me in our lowest hours. So I dwelled in a no-man's-land of unconsummated desire, constantly caught between guilt, confusion, and heady infatuation and excitement.

Michael and I—both obviously seeing what was happening between us—avoided speaking of it, as though we could simply will it away. Even though we spent time alone together, Michael never made any romantic or sexual advances toward me, instinctively understanding that if he did, I would have to put a stop to the friendship immediately.

And so we went on, falling more and more into an unspoken infatuation that eventually deepened into something more solid and real than anything I'd felt since Steve's death. *Maybe things can just stay this way*, the lie inside me whispered. *I can be a dutiful wife to Russ and yet still have this electric friendship that keeps me alive inside.* After all, Michael and I had been increasingly close for well over a year and "nothing" had happened.

If you can call falling in love "nothing."

It is hard to admit—even now, so many years later—how *stuck* I felt in my marriage to Russ. I did not want to hurt him for so, so many reasons: feeling that I owed him, that I could not do such a thing to my sons, that I did not want to be "the kind of woman" to leave her husband for another man, and even that I sincerely loved Russ as a human being. The more years I spent with him, the more I realized he was just a lost soul, and even the few outbursts of anger he had shown were driven more by confusion and overwhelm than anything resembling malice. Although Russ had grown up in a mansion on the beach in Santa Monica, the son of a wealthy and powerful man, behind those walls had been a mother he adored who suffered from severe mental illness and died young. Between that and the deaths of Tom and Steve, he had suffered a lifetime of losses, to which I could relate all too well.

When I'd started going to marital counseling, I'd told myself that I could "teach" Russ how to show love and appreciation, and to be more affectionate. In other words, I'd told myself the lie that leads to the collapse of so many marriages—that I could *change* my partner, could magically heal him of all his losses and rejections. It took me years to recognize that Russ didn't want a savior—he wanted to be accepted for who he was and had married me believing I could give him that. Maybe he even figured that we could coexist together in our mutual history of trauma and pain, not expecting much more of life, happy merely for a shelter in the storm.

Looking back with a more merciful hindsight, I see clearly that neither Russ nor I was wrong in our desires; we were simply wrong for each other. Already a middle-aged man when we met, he'd had every right to expect that any woman who married him would understand that he was set in his ways and not about to become a whole other person for anyone, not about to heal his inner wounds for my convenience.

Nor was I a monster for longing for the things I'd always experienced as normal parts of marriage. Not only had I had a decade of a mutually expressive relationship with Steve, I'd also grown up in a household full of love and affection. My parents held hands, they kissed, they sat close together on the sofa as they sipped their nightly cocktail when my father came home from work. They were my model of a traditional marriage, where husband and wife held different roles in the household and yet honored and adored one another. And while, yes, I'd been a modern, working woman when I met Steve, I was not ashamed to admit that I'd longed to be a wife, a stay-at-home mom who made a beautiful, safe, and loving home for my husband and children. Growing up, my mother had done the same for my father, and he had shown his appreciation daily. I heard the words *I love you* and *thank you* and *I appreciate you* frequently between them; I watched my mother make efforts to see that my father's homecomings after a long workday were warm and special, and I watched my father receive those efforts as she intended them and embrace her as his confidante, love, and soulmate.

Was their marriage rare in its happiness? From where I stand now, I understand that of course, yes, I was extraordinarily lucky in having such a happy marriage as a model, and just as extraordinarily lucky to find a similar joy with Steve. But I am also at a great enough distance to understand that something being "lucky" doesn't mean it is "too much to ask for." I am on the other side of enough losses and trials to understand even more than I did then that life is short—even when it is far longer than the years Steve got—and that the desire to experience happiness and reciprocity while we can is not an unpardonable crime.

And yet . . . poor Russ was a good man who had been hurt enough in one lifetime.

Both things were true. Sometimes, there is no one right answer, or even any right answer at all. I can only look back at who Russ and I were and feel a compassion for us both.

Both of us floundering. Both of us hurting, lost.

Things came to a breaking point—as things do. It was a glorious summer afternoon in early July 2006. The boys were at camp for the day and Michael invited me over for lunch.

There was nothing so unusual about this, but by this point I was beginning to accept that my relationship with him was an emotional affair, the depth of which we had to subtly shield from those around us. So, that day, I felt—though we had never touched beyond playfully slapping one another on the arm—as though some part of me was sneaking around. While once I would have thought nothing of lunch at Michael's, I was now conscious that I felt like a teenager on her first date. And I suspected that I was not alone in this feeling.

The moment I arrived at Michael's, I had my answer. As we stepped out onto his patio, which overlooked a beautiful lake, he handed me a glass of Cakebread chardonnay. Would "just a friend" (especially one who did not himself drink) have run out to buy my favorite chardonnay and had it waiting and chilled for my arrival?

He then led me to a beautifully set table. "Just sit and relax," he said. "Lunch is almost ready."

Until that moment, my mind had been buzzing loudly, full of its usual anxieties and guilt—but abruptly, my cares melted away and I felt my body and brain responding to Michael's desire to care for me. Taking in the breathtaking view, I considered that this sweet, wonderful human was inside cooking *for me*, tending to my needs, and a thrill went through me. Yes—I *was* relaxed. It felt *good* to be cared for this way. Michael was showering me with the kind of attention I so often attempted to show Russ, only to feel spurned by his disinterest.

I would not spurn Michael's efforts. Instead, I turned my face up to the sun, intent upon absorbing this caretaking in all its splendor.

As Michael appeared with an appetizing plate of salmon salad and a toasted baguette, I found myself laughing aloud with pleasure. I picked up my fork and took an indecorously large bite—only to find that the food tasted just as good as it looked.

Michael attentively refilled my wineglass as I sat taking in the view, the food, the company, feeling fully present in the moment.

As though reading my mind—a sensation I often felt with Michael—my best friend suddenly said, "Our lives certainly feel wonderful in this moment, don't they?"

I knew it was my move—that I could laugh it off as nothing or sink deeper into the romance of the moment. Gloriously, blissfully, I sank.

"Yes," I said, raising my glass to him. "If only we could stay right here; in this moment, our lives feel pretty damn perfect." And then I did something I had not planned: I stretched out and put my tanned leg up on his lap.

I had never done anything like this before, and yet Michael responded as though he found my leg resting on his every day: He wordlessly placed his hand on my foot and began to massage my insoles.

That was it. An electric current ran through my body; I could feel myself blushing hot. Our gestures were so simple, so automatic, yet it was the beginning of something new for us: the acknowledgment of our romantic connection, its realness more than mere flirtation or a crush. His touch, his conversation, everything about him set me alight. I felt both as though we could be a long-married couple and also like I was falling down the delirious chute of love for the first time. Because that is what big love gives us: a sense of newness, even when we are middle-aged, twice-married, widowed, mired in years of feeling numb inside.

When Michael leaned over and kissed me, I did not compare his kiss to Steve's or to Russ's; I didn't think of anyone or anything else at all. I was not the haunted and tragic widow; I was not the disappointed or guilty wife; I was simply *me*, some core, elemental part of myself that had been eternal since my youth, that was still capable, after everything, of the highest of highs. I was fully immersed in the moment.

Driving back to my own home after that kiss, I felt a profound sense, unlike any I had ever known, that my life was going to turn out the way it was supposed to. I still did not want to hurt Russ, but some long-buried part of myself knew that I deserved to be happy—deserved to not only think about what would be best for Brett and Colton or what might soothe my sea of grief but also to experience full-throttle joy and life lived to the fullest with a partner who wanted the exact same things.

I was so happy that, amidst my rapture, I permitted myself one last self-deception: that Russ, surely, was no more *in love* with me than I was with him, and that although we loved one another as family, there was no way he could be surprised when I told him the truth about Michael.

Maybe, the lie whispered seductively to me, *he will even be relieved.*

Confessing is easier contemplated than done. But one Friday night in August, when Russ arrived home from California, I knew I had stalled as long as my heart would allow.

That night, it may sound strange to say, I did what I always did: dressed up, put Russ's favorite beer in the fridge, and lit candles for dinner. I now understand that I was playing a kind of game with myself to garner my courage, as this time, rather than being crushed by my husband's casual greeting and lack of any compliments or thanks, I felt reassured. In my secret happiness, I took Russ's disinterest, as he sipped his beer in silence, as confirmation of my belief that he was not that invested in whether I was there or not. I would see to it that he and our sons were always close; and if Russ had come to like having a wife on some level, then surely he saw as much as I did that I was the wrong woman for the job—that to greet my husband's homecoming after a weeklong absence with just a casual, "Oh, hi," and then settle into mutually ignoring one another for the rest of our lives would never *not* feel to me like being handed the shovel to dig my own grave.

In time, I told myself, *he will realize that I'm setting him free. Somewhere out there is a quieter kind of woman who's looking for a quieter kind of companionship, and as long as Russ is with me, he will never have the gumption to go out and find her.*

I had found Michael by accident, and I genuinely wanted the same for Russ—for our struggle of clashing temperaments to end and for us both to stop having to think there was something wrong with us, respectively, for not being what the other needed.

After dinner, Brett and Colton went outside to play, and I approached Russ and asked if we could talk. I think he sensed something, because he didn't brush me off but instead gave me his full and undivided attention.

My heart was pounding, but I tried to speak clearly and kindly as I said straight out, "I have feelings for Michael." I went on to say that although Michael and I had never made love, I had long felt alone in our marriage, and that I knew I wasn't making him happy either.

It was on the tip of my tongue to tell my husband that I wanted a divorce when, for the first time in all the years I'd known him, I saw Russ Mullin break down and cry.

I was shocked. Maybe there is something in human nature that leads us to imagine that everyone else feels as we do. I was convinced that if I was deeply unhappy, surely Russ could not be more than making do himself. Instead, he was absolutely gutted. Not *angry* (which would have been easier, as we could then have descended into a game of finger-pointing and accusations as to who had bait-and-switched whom), but instead, the man who had saved my boys and me from our heartbreak was the picture of devastation.

I saw on his collapsed face that I had broken his heart—and then I, too, felt gutted. The magic of my kiss with Michael evaporated into my desperation to stop Russ's pain, and I found myself blurting the opposite of what I'd intended. "I am committed to our marriage," I promised Russ, and as the words left my lips, I realized I meant them with all my heart. His agony was unbearable to me—far more so than my own pain of the past years had been. I could not be one more person to let him down in this life, one more loss for him to endure. No, I *would* not.

As Russ sobbed in my arms, I promised I would end all communication with Michael as soon as possible.

We were both in tears. In the face of his devastation, everything I'd experienced as rejection in our marriage felt turned upside down, confusing. How could I have believed Russ didn't notice or love me, when I had never seen him have such a reaction to *anything* the way he was reacting to the thought that he could be losing me?

"I love you," I told my husband, and meant it. "This whole experience with Michael—it's just shown me that our marriage is the most important thing in my life. It's the wake-up call we needed."

I still hope we both believed me.

THE ROAD TO YESTERDAY

August 10, 2006. The woman, the mother, the mourner, the wife lingers in bed for a bit after she wakes, her heart a fist of sadness in her chest, a cool, hollow pit in her belly.

"Be grateful," she says to herself firmly, if not unkindly. "Russ is doing his best. I am doing my best."

She longs for this to be true. Last night, it seemed so true. Last night, it felt as though she was embarking on a new beginning. Why, then, when she wakes to sun streaming through her bedroom window, the sound of birds chirping and lawn mowers running outside, does she feel like she is about to go to her own funeral?

This woman is no stranger to grief. Today, she must instead remember its twin: gratitude. Even when she wept with her closest friends about losing Steve, she remembered not to overlook her gratitude for the support of her community; back when she first witnessed her beautiful boys warming up to Russ, a loving father figure ready to guide and care for them, she held close to her heart the belief that gratitude is a key component of grief's recovery, a necessary brick in the long, ever-evolving road of moving forward with meaning and purpose in the wake of a permanent loss. Or perhaps it is more appropriate to say "in the face of loss," given that her first husband's face still comes to her, unbidden, reflected in the expressions or laughter of her sons, and, of course, in her dreams, all these years later, as she lies in her bed torn between two completely other men.

How did she get here? How has it come to this? "Oh, Steve," she prays like a mantra. "Steve, I've made a mess of things. Steve, if you were here, none of this would have happened."

Sometimes gratitude is not enough. Sometimes the world still seems a bit off: The chairs are in the wrong places around the table; the weather is out of season; emotions are off-kilter.

Today is just such a day, she tells herself. There will always be such days. Her life now is with Russ. If she focuses on the facts of her story—her family's devastating loss, Russ coming to the rescue—she can almost imagine a reason for her grief that does not involve any new man, that does not involve any choice. This grief she feels so acutely today—no, it is just the same grief with whom she has grudgingly become old friends. Nothing to see here. No new hopes collapsing. No new love denied. Just familiar company.

Perhaps, the woman thinks, blinking away tears that nobody sees, she will linger in bed just a bit longer, trying to remember what brought her here—the beautiful things, the origins of her marital love. She will imagine Russ as he was when they smoked clandestinely in a hotel bar in New York, as he was when his nightly calls were what she looked forward to most of all. She will remember the promises they made to one another last night, and the promise of a bigger love that might yet flourish between them in ways she cannot yet know, because what can we really know about what comes next?

Not a lot. She learned this fact the hard way. And so: gratitude.

The woman daydreams in full-blown color about the courtship with the man who accepted and embraced her when she believed herself hollow, a hologram of a woman; the man who stepped in as a loving father; the man who chose a grieving widow with whom to make a home and a life; the man who loves her children entirely as his own. This good man who loves her, if not always in a way that is aligned with how she's imagined being loved. If she can remember their courtship, she can remember a time when there were true seeds of romantic love in those moments—those seeds must *still be here, she tells herself; if they* ever existed at all, then they can still grow into a miraculous, flowering tree.

Her mind drifts to the long-ago. *It's always safe inside a memory, where the light is flattering and the weather is perfect. The Hotel Mont-Blanc in Chamonix, with its gable roofs, its fancy fountain pens for sale in the lobby, its icy tree branches glistening in the sunshine, its gondola paths stitched like moving stars over the mountains that, when she looked at them, made her feel as though she had stepped into a living postcard. The Grand-Hotel du Cap-Ferrat on the Côte d'Azur, with its sparkling infinity pool that seemed to drop directly into the sea, disturbed only by an occasional slow-moving boat idling past. The Gritti Palace, where lovers—she and Russ among them—climbed into gondolas to slide along the canals in the wonderfully disorienting fog of love; the Villa Feltrinelli in Lake Como, where golden light fell through the stained glass, and where every picture was framed in gold.*

Honeymoons don't last, the woman tells herself, ignoring the voice that nags inside her, telling her that her parents' did, that her first marriage's did. *There is no space in this memory, in this daydream of what might still be between her and Russ, for the figure of another man whose blue eyes move her in ways even more potent than the blue waves of the Mediterranean Sea, a man who makes her feel in his presence like she is leaning toward the sun.* No: That sun was only a mirage, one that nearly swayed her to become someone unrecognizable to herself. The woman prides herself on being a good wife, a good mother, like her mother before her.

She does not want to yearn for more. She does not want to lean.

Gratitude, the woman reminds herself, knowing (better than most; better than she wishes she knew) that all days—especially this one, celebrating her firstborn son who has already *suffered so much loss; and then the next day, with its untold comings and goings—contain within them possibilities that can only be encountered or uncovered if you* face *that world. Nobody has a crystal ball, she reminds herself, and in a moment of levity she laughs aloud: Who would want one? Who would ever get out of bed again if they knew?*

And then, because she is a mother who loves her son, and it is his birthday, and to celebrate him fills her with a bright, unwavering light; and because she is a widow who still loves her first husband and his loss, only five years ago, is the undercurrent beneath her life, a steady pulse that reminds her to rise to her higher self; and because she is a wife who loves her second husband and wants to make him happy; and because she is a mourner—always a mourner of what was lost and what might never be—she gets out of bed and moves into the day.

It is her son's birthday, yes, but it is also, for her, a day of reckoning—the closing, forever, of a door that, just for a brief while, seemed to beckon her back toward the sun.

On Brett's birthday, August 10, I woke with two intentions: to celebrate my son and to call Michael and tell him that I couldn't see or talk to him anymore. I hugged Brett and told him I loved him. My smile felt plastered on my face.

Russ, who could hardly look at me, took the boys out all day, but come evening we had a cake for Brett, my perceptive young man who later admitted he knew something was amiss—felt intuitively that this was not going to be his best birthday.

No sooner had he blown out his candles than his stepfather, who by now was no less his real father than Steve had been, and I made the surprise announcement that we would return to California the next day.

"But, Mom," Brett whined momentarily, "summer isn't over yet."

Does my memory play tricks on me, though, or did his complaints end there, the looks on Russ's and my faces silencing him into acquiescence?

Looking at him, and at young Colton, I remembered why I was about to do something that felt like cutting off my own hand. For my sons, I reminded myself, I would do that and more. To save Russ from experiencing the crushing pain he had last night, I would do that and more. *I had my time in the sun*, I told myself. *I had my decade with Steve—more joy than most people get in a lifetime. I had the thrill of falling in love with Michael. We shared one perfect kiss I will be able to feel on my lips until the day I die. Don't be greedy. You and Russ may never have what you had with Steve, what you could have had with Michael, but you can still turn this around and make it work.*

Saying goodbye to Michael was excruciating. Russ and I sat side by side in the living room, the boys asleep in their beds, and though I knew Russ and I were, as a married couple, a team, I could not stop feeling like I was betraying Michael for what I was about to do, for the callousness of making our goodbye public—for Russ had asked me to put the call on speakerphone so he could believe me, so he could hear for himself that it was over, and I could not deny him this entirely reasonable request. He was my husband, after all!

Still, with this small act, I knew, too, that I was losing my best friend, the knower of my deepest feelings and the keeper of my deepest confidences. I was drawing a line clearly in the sand: him on one side, and Russ and me together on ours.

"Michael," I said in a voice more formal than the one we'd come to use with one another, "I need you to know that you are on speakerphone right now and Russ and I are here together." It was the least I could do, to let him know his words would be heard by my husband, to let him choose how much he wanted to reveal of his feelings in this vulnerable circumstance; and yet I also knew that by telling him up front, I was denying both of us the chance to speak freely. "Russ and I are going back to California tomorrow morning with the boys to work on our marriage. I'm rededicating myself to my family, and you and I will not be in communication anymore."

I would never see Michael's face as he received this news, never see if my words caused the sparkle I so loved to leave his eyes. I would never know if the grief on his countenance was similar to what I had witnessed the night before with Russ. Maybe I didn't want to know.

"I understand, Maryellen," Michael said stoically, kindly. "Of course, you need to do what is right for you and your family." His voice cracked then, and he was silent for a long moment while my heart hammered through my summer dress. "I wish you both every happiness," he said, his voice thick with tears, and then he hung up the phone.

The lump in my throat was so enormous I could not speak. I willed myself not to weep in front of Russ—it would be disrespectful, cruel. I wanted to tear my hair from my head, but instead I sat impassive, my eyes downcast.

It was finished. No matter what my sons thought, summer was gone.

Russ agreed to couple's counseling, but during the single session we had with a therapist, he literally didn't say a word. I sat beside him in our session, as I had when ending things with Michael, accepting my role as the wife who had strayed, the would-be homewrecker.

Perhaps our therapist thought Russ was within his right to hold his tongue—that it was part of my penance—but I knew better: Russ was not punishing me or acting out. This was simply who he was. I'd learned it as early as our honeymoon in Hawaii, and it had been reinforced at every stage of our marriage, in every new home and location. Yet I had convinced myself that because he'd shed tears over the thought of losing me, somehow everything would change.

Wasn't the very fact of coming to terms with his repressed nature what had led me to fall in love with Michael to begin with—hadn't I already learned that people do not change?

My hands shook with restraint until we left the therapist's office and headed to our car.

Even alone, Russ had nothing to say for himself.

"Well," I said in exasperation, "are you going to speak the next time we go, or am I still basically going to counseling by myself?"

"I'm sorry," Russ said.

Every cell in my body waited for him to explain his nonparticipation.

"I can't do that again, Mare," he said simply. "It's just not my thing."

I was so angry in that moment that I, too, lost the ability to speak, for fear of what might come out of my mouth. We drove in silence back to our house.

Although we had been back in California for several weeks already, absolutely nothing between us had changed. If anything, my admission about Michael had put me in the role of the wrongdoer, and so perhaps it was even easier for Russ to tell himself that he was not the one who needed to do anything differently.

Was he correct? Had I lost what few rights I might have once possessed to demand more of my marriage?

Russ and I fell asleep that night with no heart-to-heart talk, no passionate make-up sex, nothing except the silence that, now that I had revealed my truths, was no longer even "companionable" but instead full of tension.

Listening to Russ's breath rising and falling in sleep, I lay in the dark engulfed by a terrible sadness the likes of which I had not felt since before we were together, when Steve's loss was still fresh and naked. As I had then, I felt drained of all hope. Russ wasn't going to be a man who expressed his feelings to a counselor, and he wasn't going to work on the wedge that had formed between us. I had lost Michael as my confidant, and I had consigned myself to a lifetime of emotional loneliness in the name of duty and obligation. There was nowhere to go from here.

At that time, it was impossible for me to imagine the inner life of the man sleeping deeply in retreat on the other side of the bed. I see him now, though, so clearly that if I close my eyes I can almost feel the way our old bed molded itself to his body. I can almost hear the voice inside his head—the voice of his father—telling him he was never as worthy as Tom. I feel the dreadful confusion he must have experienced as he tried to navigate life—after losing his mother, his brother, his stepbrother, the company he thought would be his, and even his bachelorhood and independence—free-falling as a husband of a dissatisfied woman and father of two active young boys, without the skills or confidence to be the man he was trying to be for us. Inside the swirl of his head, the voice telling him that his father didn't trust him with Tom's leadership role, that he was not magically strong enough to save his mother, that even the widowed woman he believed he *had* saved found him lacking...

The voices feel so deafening that I now understand why Russ's only response was silence. It was, quite simply, too much for him—and who understood that better than I, when, frankly, our cumulative losses were too much for *all* of us?

All we could do was do our best to cope and keep showing up for one another in whatever ways we were capable of. There were no villains here, just ordinary people trying to be their best selves.

And so, that is what we did. We focused on the boys, Russ grew more withdrawn, and I felt like a shell of myself until that, too, began to feel familiar.

That fall, Russ lost a lot of weight, quickly. He had a persistent cough, and his immune system couldn't seem to fight it off. I blamed myself, thinking I had caused him undue stress that was impacting his health—after all, I, too, had lost much of my appetite and zeal for life, and I didn't imagine that Michael, whatever he was doing, was enjoying salmon salad in the sun or pouring wine for another woman in a romantic fervor either. I had wreaked havoc on our lives, and it would take time for us all to recover.

But when Russ's symptoms became increasingly severe, my self-blaming narrative—in which I was so powerful that I had the single-handed ability to turn my previously healthy husband into a borderline invalid—floundered. I was not so powerful, I knew. Something was genuinely *wrong*. And although I had promised myself that I was done making demands of Russ, I made one final demand: that he go to the doctor for a checkup.

It was October 11, 2006: both Russ's and Colton's birthdays. I was at the bakery picking up cupcakes for Colton's class when I got the call. Russ had finally come from a doctor's appointment after my begging him for weeks to go.

His words hit me like I was standing in my kitchen with Kenny on the other end of the line five years and one month earlier and standing in a busy bakery with a giant box of cupcakes in my hands at once. As though my body had divided into a split screen, one with Kenny saying bleakly, "Turn on the TV," and one holding my cell phone in sunny California as I heard my husband, Steve's stepbrother, uttering the words "stage IV lung cancer."

These days, this diagnosis, though still devastating, can contain nuances and intricacies it did not in 2006. Now, nearly twenty years later, there are long-term survivors who can live for a decade—or more—with late-stage cancer, sometimes even with all traces of illness eliminated from their systems. These days, a diagnosis is often followed by prolonged uncertainty as treatments commence: whose cases will turn out to be terminal vs. who will go on to live vibrant, pleasurable lives.

Back then, this was not the case. Back then, as many who have lost a loved one to cancer know, there was generally one outcome, and it was usually swift.

So it was that our family faced our biggest hurdle since our world was torn apart on 9/11: telling our sons that their second father did not have long to live.

Bravely, subjugating whatever fears raged in his own heart, Russ put all self-concern aside as he spoke to each boy separately. I will never forget my darling Brett, not even a teenager yet, running to me with tears streaming down his face, throwing his arms around me, and yelling, "How can this be happening?"

How indeed? The split screen appeared again as I saw my child five years earlier, at the candlelight vigil our old neighbors in Connecticut held for Steve, and now here, an adolescent weeping in his mother's embrace, another father's loss already preordained. All we could do was face it as a family. If I had ever possessed doubt (and I had—I *had*) that I'd done the right thing in cutting things off with Michael, I saw now with a singular vision that my place was at Russ's side.

Russ began chemo immediately—an attempt to buy any extra time he possibly could with our sons. Trying to keep things as normal as possible for the boys, we even went on our annual trip to Mazatlán with the Ziggerses. It was an emotional time for all of us, as even by then Russ had gotten so weak that we knew this would be our last trip together.

Although we didn't know it yet, and at the time never would have believed it even possible, there would be yet another layer to this catastrophe soon. Real life is not a movie set, and so in real life, truth can be stranger and more brutal than fiction. There is no director to yell, "Cut!" or writer's room to ask one another, "Hey, do you think this is overload—will the audience even believe this shit?" There is only our small, transient humanity, our bodies blowing in the wind of fate, free to be knocked over again and again.

And if love is a bright, unwavering light, as I believe it is, we would need it now more than ever before.

CHAPTER 8
LIGHTNING STRIKES THRICE

My only purpose, during the ensuing months, was to take care of my husband. There were so many potential ways to feel about this, and intellectually I understood them all. I'd left Michael, with whom I knew I could be happy, to return to California with a husband who would not even go to therapy or do anything to shift the dynamic in our marriage. Upon now learning that Russ was terminally ill, I suppose I could have felt bitter, angry, resentful. I could have wrung my hands, remembering Steve's death, and thought, *Why me? Why do these terrible things keep happening to me?*

Don't get me wrong; I was no saint. I knew life wasn't fair, and there were dark moments when I had some of these thoughts. But overall, something far more unexpected happened after Russ's diagnosis. Somehow, in the face of his grueling illness, my long-estranged husband and I rediscovered our deep friendship.

Even more surprisingly? We began to have a hell of a good time.

In the absence of striving to feel a romantic connection that had never quite found its legs, I began to remember why Russ had been such a comfort to me once, after Steve's death, and to feel genuine gratitude for the opportunity to be that comfort to him now, in his darkest hours.

Perhaps the most surprising thing of all, actually, was how *not dark* so many of those early hours were. Russ was, above all things, a realist. He had none of the delusions or denial that some face when they are given grave diagnoses; he didn't scramble or freak out or take to his bed in a depression. Instead, his zeal for life resurfaced.

As Russ would explain it to me later, before our marriage he had been "dead already"; having lost his brother to melanoma, the company he believed he would someday helm, and even his stepbrother, all while living the life of a lonely and introverted bachelor, he'd felt he had nothing left to live for. When he and I had first connected and become a couple, we'd both been at the lowest moments of our lives.

"You gave me something to live for," he told me. "I became a father."

Parenting our sons had been the joy of his life, an unexpected second act he'd never even dreamed of finding until we stumbled, aimless and numb, into each other's arms. And though we hadn't been the right fit romantically—though I had no more been the right woman for Russ than he had been the right man for me—through me, he had found his one true calling: fatherhood.

There at the edge of the abyss, knowing he had scant time left, all of Russ's and my grievances against one another melted away. His unexpected second act was proving much shorter than we had ever imagined: He would not be at our sons' graduations or weddings, see the birth of any children. But Russ did not linger on these could-have-beens. Instead, he praised his luck at having found meaning and purpose before he was to depart the earth, and he now had one agenda and one agenda only until that day came: to have a hell of a good time.

As such, Russ rarely went in to work anymore. Rather, he would often sleep in, then at 10:30 or 11:00 a.m. suddenly pronounce, "Let's drink champagne!" And so, we would! Nothing but the good stuff, either; given our 9/11 settlement, it was clear the boys and I would be all right, so there was no reason to sit on Russ's money or senselessly hoard it. He wanted to spend it having as high a time as he could while he was still strong enough to enjoy life.

One day, he went to a Lexus dealer and asked to see the nicest car on the lot. He had always driven a beat-up Ford Explorer, but that day he left the dealership with a sleek, black, sexy Lexus that he took to driving 100 miles per hour along the ocean highway that wound through the mountains north of Santa Monica. On the days Brett and Colton drove that 120-mile stretch with him, they were both terrified and thrilled, their father seeming wild and invincible even as he stared death in the face. Though, looking back, my heart races at the thought of my sons in that speeding car, I suppose in truth we all felt a kind of surreal sense of invincibility during the months we spent waiting for Russ to decline further. His end felt predetermined, and superstitiously, perhaps, it seemed nothing else could touch him—or the boys or me, while we were by his side—in the meanwhile.

Armed with his new carpe diem attitude, Russ also began smoking twice his normal amount. We knew—of course we knew—what his doctors and many others would say about that and the judgmental ideas they might hold, but I didn't judge Russ in the least.

"Fuck it," he said. "I'm going to do whatever the hell I want to do. I'm dying no matter what."

I didn't begrudge him his vices. I saw that Russ was facing death on his own terms, and sometimes grief welled up in me that Steve had never had the chance to do that. Then I would remember the squawk box and think of Steve's voice saying he was going to round up the young mothers in the office and take them to safety, and the lump in my throat would swell so that I could barely breathe or swallow. Steve had died as he'd lived—had gone out exemplifying the true essence of himself.

In comparison, Russ and I were the lucky ones: We did not have to grapple with heroism or the deaths of thousands of others simultaneously while navigating his illness. We had the beautiful chance to give Death the middle finger—living every day like it was our last, lingering over extravagant lunches at the Four Seasons, where we (literally) ordered every kind of sushi on the menu.

I felt privileged to be Russ's faithful sidekick during his adventures. He was so alive—admittedly, I sometimes thought that if only he had embraced life so fully before he was dying, maybe our marriage could have been a different beast entirely. But that didn't matter now. That he had never been more awake than he was in these months would end up meaning the entire world to me, topped only by the fact that during these months we were best friends again, the way we'd been years prior when we'd talked on the phone every night. Somehow, along the way, we'd forgotten how much *fun* it was possible to have together, and how much we enjoyed one another's company.

During these months, we didn't rekindle our romance, but we were more affectionate and loving toward one another. We hugged and held hands and talked easily and amicably.

If I thought about Michael during this time, it was only in the context of feeling relief that I had not actually left Russ prior to his diagnosis—that he knew I had chosen him, even when I believed our marriage would last another few decades, and not that "'til death do us part" would become so literal so soon.

Then, the unthinkable happened.

It began with an irregular mammogram. Perhaps in the same way I believed Russ invulnerable to the winding mountain roads, I did not worry much at first when I was brought in for further testing. My husband was dying of stage IV cancer after my first husband had been killed in a terrorist attack; my getting cancer, too, would be like some kind of absurd satire.

But suddenly, there I was, diagnosed with stage II breast cancer that had spread locally to my lymph nodes. Russ and I could not even believe it—but my two-time mother-in-law, Sharon, wasted zero time before putting me in touch with surgeons at both Sloan Kettering and Johns Hopkins.

One surgeon told me I needed only a lumpectomy; the other declared that I should have a total mastectomy. All at once, the fear set in. Though Russ and I had been living high on the hog, thumbing our noses at Death, we were only human and had both faced enough loss already for two lifetimes. How could it even be real that now I was sick too—that I needed surgery, radiation? How could it be that I was now in the position of burdening Russ with my own health needs when I was supposed to be his support person, his fearless sidekick, as he careened toward his meeting with his maker?

And, of course, what about the boys?

In my fear, I reached out one day to Michael, to whom I hadn't spoken in months. Rekindling our affair was the last thing on my mind—and the last thing on his, too, once he heard all my news. I called him because I trusted him and knew he would never wish any ill upon me, knew he was not the type of man who lost his care for a woman the moment she wasn't "his." I needed someone to talk to, even just once, who could withstand my terror and grief.

Just as I knew he would be, Michael was there for me. He listened . . . and he had advice.

"There's someone I would trust with my life," he told me. "She's who you should see."

Dr. Alice Police was a surgeon at Hoag Hospital. On Michael's referral, I made an appointment, and once more was reminded that who each of us is to one another is so complex, transcending labels like "emotional affair" or even "husband and wife." Just as I had given Russ the greatest gift of his life with our sons, even though I was not a perfect wife, so Michael, whom I'd never expected to see again, gave me Alice, who would shepherd me through the minefield of breast cancer and become one of the most valuable relationships of my life.

Dr. Police—or Alice, as she became known to me—had none of the arrogance or detachment that is legendary in surgeons; she was warm, nurturing, and utterly brilliant. Under her care, I underwent a lumpectomy and then—in another surreal twist—Russ and I began an eight-week course of radiation together in Los Angeles. I had, alas, become Russ's sidekick in the most unexpected of ways, and this became one more adventure—if not one we would ever have chosen—that we went through together. Our radiation team told us they had never before had a husband-wife pair at the same time; it was a dubious honor we both could have lived without, and yet we learned to laugh about it too. Sometimes, there is nothing else to do but laugh.

It was beyond bizarre to endure eight weeks of radiation together—our past, left behind when we returned to California, now felt like a dream. Instead of either the sad estrangement we'd been living or the idealized marital bliss of my imagination, now we were some kind of poster couple for fighting cancer. But "fighting" meant such different things for each of us. For me, the only side effect of radiation was occasional tiredness. For Russ, who was going through chemo at the same time, it took a far more brutal toll.

It was extremely hard for Brett and Colton to see their father declining so rapidly, and hard for me, during this time, to remember that the point of all this was to buy Russ some more quality time once treatment had finished. I know we both wondered at times if it was worth it, and yet Russ did what most parents of young children would do: every damn thing possible to extend his life for the sake of his sons.

Brett and Colton, who had been through too much already, put on brave faces for their father, but when each time they went to say goodbye to Russ in the morning before school and found him lying there with bunches of hair on his pillow, I thought my body would crack from its deep ache for them—for us all.

My breast now had a scar from the lumpectomy, and the radiation ravaged Russ's skin, reminding us both that our youthful, healthy bodies—for we had both been lucky enough to even have the kind of able bodies that required little thought or effort to begin with—had only ever been on loan to us.

Life, we were learning, is all about finding the people who will hold you up and be at your side when those bodies seem to betray you. Though Russ and I had failed at so much else, in this we succeeded—and that, in the end, was everything.

There are endless details of any individual struggle with cancer, but in the end, this is not the story of my cancer. What I didn't know then was that eight years later, Russ already long gone, I would face breast cancer for the second time, this time having one of my breasts removed and undergoing chemotherapy, again under Dr. Police's expert care. I did not know that I would have to tell my sweet young sons that I was sick again and returning to California to have my single mastectomy. I did not know that upon hearing this news Colton, only fourteen, would insist on being by my side at all my appointments, meeting with doctors and hearing every update. I did not know I would need to be close to the hospital for six weeks as I faced this grisly saga on repeat, only intensified by recurrence. I did not know, of course, that now, at the time of writing this story, I would be cancer-free for nearly ten years, nor did I know all of the things that could fill a whole other book with information I learned, connections I made, wisdom I heard from other women who had been through similar juggernauts. I did not yet understand that, although no one would ever choose to have cancer, I would end up changed as a result in ways I would not trade, so intrinsic would they become to who I am. I did not know how often I would recall Russ and the passion with which he'd seized life by the horns while looking his mortality in the eyes, and how he would become my teacher even once he was no longer part of this world.

In 2007, I knew only that I had been given a second chance at life—a chance Russ would never have—and that we celebrated my survival together, even as we realized he would not be around to see what I would make of it and who I might become, a no-longer-young woman living on without him. And if love is to be able to look full in the face at a thing you will never have—the most important thing of all, *life*—and yet rejoice that someone else *will* have that chance, then that alone showed me the depth of Russ's love for me in ways I wish I had understood during the dark and lonely years of our marriage, before I turned to Michael. I did not always feel loved when Russ and I were a couple, and I now understand that Russ didn't either, despite my strident efforts to be a "good wife" as I understood it: the kind of wife my father had so appreciated; the kind of wife I had been with Steve. If only Russ and I had understood one another as well in health as we did, later, in sickness.

Realizing all this, I began to understand that sometimes the vow "in sickness and in health" is meant to convey that *health* constitutes the good times, the easy times, and yet it is not always that way at all. Sometimes it is only in sickness that we are able to slow down, stop trying to fit ourselves and others into the pictures in our heads, and learn to appreciate people as full individuals—as complete and enough, just as they are. In health, Russ and I had proven incapable of doing that. In sickness, we grieved, we raged, we cried, but also, we laughed, we celebrated, we loved. And he cheered me on though he knew a train would soon pull up to take him away and I would remain standing on the platform after its departure, left behind to live for us both—and for Steve too.

I held them both, stepbrothers who had loved one another, deep in my soul as I prepared to stand on that solitary platform, waiting for the train to leave without me, to take my second husband somewhere I could—thankfully, miraculously—not yet follow.

Marriage is a complex beast. Although, until his illness, Russ and I had been the opposite of "close," he had nonetheless managed during the years of our marriage to form a beautiful and intimate relationship with my beloved father. "Your dad is more of a father to me than my own ever has been" was a comment Russ made frequently—and so, not knowing how much longer he would be able to travel, we planned one final gathering with my family in Florida.

We all celebrated New Year's Eve together at the Don CeSar hotel in St. Petersburg, Florida, just a couple hours away from where Mom and Dad now lived. I brimmed with both pride and grief that my entire clan understood the gravity of this trip and so there was perfect attendance, despite how busy everyone's lives were: All three of my brothers came, along with their wives and children. Everyone understood that Russ would not be at 100 percent, that he was exhausted much of the time; our focus was simply being together. Even Mom, though far enough into dementia that she could no longer be left alone, knew enough of why we were all gathered to understand the implications.

THE ROAD TO YESTERDAY

I had always been proud of my family of origin, but never more so than on this trip. Especially valuable to me was that they didn't take the lens off Russ to cluck and fuss about my own diagnosis, which—even in 2007—gave overwhelming odds in favor of my long-term survival. While I was still a daddy's girl and my brothers' baby sister, I wanted the focus to be on Russ, and they abided my decision.

What is there to say of this trip? To recount what we ate and drank would feel slightly obscene. Although it was supposed to be a festive time of year, it was obviously grueling on everyone, especially when it came time for us to all depart for our separate corners of the world again.

Our facade of celebration cracked as my parents and brothers and sisters-in-law hugged Russ goodbye. It was New Year's Day, but for Russ, this meaning had become its own inverse: It was the last New Year's Day he would ever see; the last time he would set foot in Florida; the last time he would shake my father's hand, then fall into an embrace with him.

How strange it is to say goodbye to someone who is still among the living, still walking and cracking jokes, and know that you will never see them alive again. Is it better to have such knowledge—as we did with Russ—or not to have it, as had been the case with Steve?

Russ and I cherished having the time to prepare, to put things in order—between ourselves, most of all—and yet a bandage hurts even more when pulled off slowly, taking with it bits of skin.

By the time Russ was saying his final goodbyes to my family in Florida, my father had been coping with my mother's dementia for years. She would survive Russ by more than seven years, declining all the while—a decline that had already started before Steve's young life was snuffed out in an instant. It is only now, as an older woman, that I see how I looked at my parents' "good years"—of which there were, mercifully, many—as such a guidepost for me and what I wanted of marriage, and yet it was probably the way my father cared for my mother for some fifteen years as, piece by piece, she slowly slipped away from him that taught me more about love than anything else ever could. How many times, over the years, did my brothers and I beg my father, for both his and our mother's good, to put her into assisted living so she couldn't slip and fall on the marble floor, get lost while he was sleeping, or unwittingly destroy what remained of his health as he cared for her—something she would never have allowed when she was in full possession of her faculties and wanted nothing more than my father's happiness. And yet the only time in my life I ever heard my father raise his voice was the day he screamed at my brothers and me, "Enough! She is my wife! I take care of her, and I will not be told what to do!"

Even when moving into assisted living became utterly necessary for her own safety, my father went to eat meals with her daily.

"She doesn't know you," her own doctors tried to tell him kindly. "You don't need to come every single day."

And my father, with quiet dignity, said to the doctors as though they understood nothing, "But I know *her*."

When my mother at last was released from the long, cruel ordeal of dementia and died in 2015, my wise brother David tried to urge our dad into a facility, saying, "Dad, I don't want you to open a can of soup every night"—but our proud and independent father flatly refused. Only when he underwent a minor eye surgery and ended up with an infection, leading his doctor to refuse to release him on his own recognizance, did he finally move into assisted living.

There, the gender gap of life expectancy being what it is, my father could have been like a rooster at a hen party, so in demand was he among the spry women residents. He never took the slightest interest. "There is and has always been one love of my life," he told me.

He lasted three years without my mother before slipping away in 2018. I hope they were rejoined in an eternity where neither would ever want for anything more, for theirs was a true love—sixty-five years of a connection that never wavered, that could not be threatened by anything dished out by life or even death.

This was the love story that had taught me how to love Steve, taught me what to expect or even demand of marriage. This was the love story that had led me to conclude that what I had with Russ was not enough and had urged me toward Michael's arms.

Now, I understand that it was also the love story that taught me how to shepherd Russ to his death without flinching, to remain at his side till the end.

As the writer Gina Frangello wrote in one of her novels, in which 9/11 features prominently, "There is never only one Truth. There is only one truth at a time."

And in that spirit:

One night in April, Russ and I were having dinner when he turned to me and said, "I want to have a conversation with Michael."

My heart skipped several hundred beats. Although Michael had helped me to find Dr. Police, for which Russ and I were both grateful, I tried for the most part to believe that Russ had forgotten about our nearly running off together, as though the cancer had ravaged not only his body but also his mind.

I set my fork down, tried to chew slowly to buy myself some time. Russ Mullin was an incredibly intelligent man whose still waters ran deep, and I knew that if I tried to say something banal—to brush Michael off as some fantasy that had meant nothing, for example—he would see right through me. My husband knew I was not the type of woman who would have a "fling."

Though to me it felt like decades had passed since that glorious lunch on Michael's deck where we'd shared an unforgettable kiss, in reality it had been less than a year. Further, Russ had known Michael as long as I had—he was no phantom in the wings; he was a former friend and golf buddy. Of *course* Russ had not forgotten.

"Are you sure you want that?" I asked, careful to neither infantilize him nor try to steer him away from what he might need.

"Yes," he said, resting his hand on mine as if to let me know I had nothing to fear.

And so I learned yet another lesson about love.

"I don't have long," I heard my husband say to my would-be-lover, "and I know you love Maryellen."

My husband wanted to make sure I would be all right.

He wanted to make sure he had not irreparably torn the connection between me and the man I loved.

He wanted to give us his blessing.

He was not wrong: I *was* still in love with Michael, though I rarely let myself think of him. What had blossomed between us for nearly two years could not fade away in a matter of months.

Yet also: I had never loved Russ more.

After that conversation, I began to speak again to Michael, and he resumed his place as my sounding board and confidant. Out of respect for Russ—and for our sons, who continue to love him as a father even after death—I'm not including my recollections of any of my conversations with Michael here in this book. During that time, we were in different states, and my life was in Los Angeles with Russ as we moved through a series of "lasts," including his last Father's Day with our sons, as well as his own father, whom Russ loved despite their difficult relationship. My one purpose was to be at Russ's side until the end—and perhaps, in his wisdom and generosity, he knew that to best accomplish that, I needed not to be tossed into the deep end of the trauma pool as I had been when the boys and I lost Steve. I needed to have someone in my corner who could absorb the storm of me. I had that, and I am forever grateful to Russ for making it possible.

My parents had shown me one perfect version of love: Boy meets girl, they fall in love, they marry, they carry on in their beautiful love until they are both old and even beyond, to the grave.

That would not be my story.

I'd had an affair with a married man when I was only twenty-five years old. Most estimates put the rate of extramarital affairs that actually end in marriage themselves at somewhere between 3 and 5 percent and the divorce rate of such marriages as being as high as 75 percent. Thankfully, Steve and I defied those odds.

Still, I had already buried one husband before the age of forty-one.

I then fell, far too fast, into the arms of my husband's stepbrother, largely at the orchestration of my well-intended-if-a-bit-controlling stepmother, and as quickly as it had seemed my salvation, it had begun to feel like a trap.

And so I'd strayed, this time not the mistress but the adulterer, into the arms of another.

Then I'd left Michael in a fugue of confusion and guilt, my marriage to Russ continuing to seem doomed even after I'd chosen him and disavowed my lover.

And now my husband and lover had spoken as gentlemen who both wanted the best for me, who could put their differences aside, who were willing to rise above competition and ownership.

Did I even deserve such generosity?

Maybe I deserved it no more than I "deserved" three miscarriages or the tragedy of 9/11 or a double feature of cancer. Maybe the very idea of *what we deserve* is part of a toxic myth.

I did not have my parents' perfect love story.

Instead, I had three.

Each vastly different. Two of which ended with life-splitting pain as I said goodbye to the men I loved and remained behind to comfort the boys who'd also loved them.

My third love story was still mostly unwritten. And for now, we will leave it there, as I continued to live my second, with strange and unexpected overlaps.

But I will say this: I would not give up any of the three for the world.

As the saying goes, things fall apart in two ways: gradually, and then all at once. Russ and I had been in the midst of his semi-gradual decline for some eight months already when one day he said to me, "Mare, you know what I'd really love to do? We had some of our best times in Europe. I'd love to see it one more time."

It hadn't occurred to me that Russ might feel up to that level of travel; as soon as he suggested it, I jumped at the chance to help him plan a bucket-list dream trip. We had mutual, deeply fond memories of our times together in Europe, back when we were first falling in love. It was strange to think back on those times as "innocent"—after all, they'd taken place just after I lost Steve in the most infamous terrorist attack in history—but now I understood that lost innocence can mean so many things. The versions of ourselves that Russ and I had been on our fabulous European vacations were versions who had not yet disappointed one another or ourselves. Just as I ached with guilt, still, for the pain I'd put Russ through over Michael, I knew that Russ, even though he wasn't one to articulate his complex feelings, regretted not having tried harder to be the kind of involved and interactive husband I'd longed for. We both wished we'd done better by the other.

Although we had come to a remarkable place of peace since Russ's conversation with Michael, still, the thought of returning to Europe and recapturing some of who we'd both been back then filled me with a kind of advance nostalgia. This would be the trip I would have to look back on once Russ was gone, I knew. It would confirm that our marriage, while it had not been the stuff of dreams, was going out on a high note—one of total acceptance of the other for who we both were. We quickly settled on our mutually beloved Italy and France and began making plans for one last hurrah.

We began—where else?—in Rome. Our hotel was at the top of the Spanish Steps, one of our favorite parts of the city. But no sooner were we there than I regretted our choice of location. Walking up the 135 steps to reach our hotel was grueling for Russ—what had, all these months, seemed a slow decline started to accelerate the moment we found ourselves in a not-very-accessible, old-world city full of steep stone staircases and cobblestoned, narrow streets.

Hovering anxiously, I suggested to Russ, exhausted from our climb, that we order in room service and relax, but Russ—soft-spoken but tough as nails—wouldn't hear of it.

"We're in Rome!" he said, and so off we went.

I insisted we not descend back to the Piazza di Spagna, at the base of the Spanish Steps, and instead to stay near the Piazza Trinità dei Monti at the top of the steps, under the shadow of the gleaming white Trinità dei Monti Roman Catholic church, with its two regal towers that could not help but remind me—despite the wildly different architecture and environment—of the Twin Towers in Manhattan, giving me a sudden chill of doom: Here, under the watchful eyes of the church towers, yet another husband of mine was dying.

I shook the thought from my head, made the sign of the cross quickly, and chose to re-spin my darker thoughts into faith that God—whatever God was—was watching over Russ and me and that in the shadow of this spectacular church, no harm could befall us.

Thankfully, even without descending into the spectacular and always bustling Piazza di Spagna, we soon found a picturesque ristorante and sat down, not speaking of our mutual relief at having made it to a destination in one piece.

My relief came too soon. For although the food was delicious, Russ was feeling nauseous and worn down and only picked at his plate. Outside, walking back to our hotel, he suddenly moved rapidly from my side to lean against a building, where he uncontrollably threw up what scant bit of his meal he'd managed to get down at dinner.

I rushed to his side—Russ was nothing if not a dignified man, and I was sure such a public display of "weakness" would normally be devastating to him. But he shrugged it off.

"Well," he quipped, "plenty of room in me for breakfast, then—they'd better have a massive buffet!"

In these terrible weeks in which Russ's "gradual" decline suddenly veered to "all at once," I watched my husband let go of the ego and concerns about image that haunt so many of us for most of our lives. Russ was not about to waste any of his remaining time lamenting.

I laughed, if weakly.

We returned to our hotel room, and I stood at the window surveying all the young people languishing on the Spanish Steps—the Vespas whizzing by in the piazza below; the couples walking arm in arm or pausing to kiss; the late-night partiers clinking their wineglasses together at outdoor cafés. We had come to Italy to live it up one last time, but Russ and I were already removed from that world. We existed, now, on another side of a veil—or rather, Russ did, and I stood beside him, still able to look out into the world I would rejoin once he was gone.

The grief was overwhelming. How could Russ die just as we were finally coming to truly understand one another? But again, I shook off my anxieties. I was not here to make this trip about me and my worries. I was here to make sure Russ had the best time he possibly could, and if he was not going to let the challenges get him down, I refused to do so either.

And indeed, Russ remained undaunted. The next morning, as we had breakfast outside in the hotel's lovely courtyard, he suddenly called the maître d' over to our table and asked, all smiles and charm, "Tell me, is your Presidential Suite by any chance available?"

"I will go and check immediately, sir," the maître d' said.

Soon, he was back to confirm that indeed the hotel's Presidential Suite was vacant. Russ arranged to have our things transferred from our room to the magnificent suite while we luxuriated in the sun, sipping our coffees. We did not even ask what the Presidential Suite cost. Russ still planned to spend all his money before he left this planet, and though his money was definitely finite—he was not the Mr. Money Bags his father was—it seemed his time was increasingly finite too. Bring on the extravagance!

I did not know, then, that Russ was teaching me how to live in a new way. Although my parents were financially secure, they were rarely extravagant, even when they could afford to be. And while I'd had tastes of Sharon's wildly glamorous lifestyle through my marriage to her son and stepson, it had normally been my default, when left to my own devices, to be "sensible" about money like my parents, my role models in almost all ways. I knew I could not go through life just ordering champagne at 11:00 a.m. and staying in every Presidential Suite I encountered, but I was learning a lot from Russ about living in the moment. I would be less cautious going forward, even when it occasionally defied "common sense."

Now a two-time cancer survivor who has buried two husbands, I don't hesitate to seize a moment of luxury, even if I know I'll spend some time paying off a bit of debt. I've stopped thinking of money as something to hoard for a rainy day. I've learned—through my marriages to Steve and Russ, through my own experiences with cancer—that *any* day may suddenly call for rain, that we may lose the chance to enjoy our lives unexpectedly and abruptly. I watched Russ become more alive than he had ever been while his body was dying, and I understood that no matter who we are, no matter our economic situation (obviously not everyone can dash off to Italy and stay in the best room of the hotel), living life to its fullest can often mean letting go of a scarcity mindset, of living in fear and preparation rather than in the now. I vowed, watching my husband behave in ways that might appear utterly irrational to some people, to learn from him, and I did.

After Rome, Russ and I set off for a destination new to me: Eze, a town in the Provence-Alpes-Côte d'Azur region of southeastern France.

Eze rises from a glistening blue sea ascending up spiraling roads to a medieval hilltop village. With fewer than three thousand residents, it was both the complete antithesis of the bustling, loud (if spectacular) chaos of Rome and also a stunning heaven on earth. I could feel my body relaxing as we settled in for our five days of total rest, relaxation, and—I presumed—tranquil seclusion.

But my indominable husband had other plans! We'd been at our hotel barely a few hours when Russ began gregariously chatting with another couple at the hotel, a Midwestern husband and wife in their fifties, and invited them to join us for drinks.

An extrovert by nature, I was of course delighted to meet new people, but I had to laugh to myself: When Russ was perfectly able-bodied and younger, I'd had to wage war to get him to so much as attend a block party—now, he was befriending random strangers when he was so weak that he had been throwing up in the streets of Rome! Oh, the things that had seemed so life-and-death at the time, that horrible and ridiculous row Russ and I had had over that block party . . . how I wished I could go back in time and somehow find more understanding in my heart for his shyness, his demons. Only now, at the edge of the abyss, did such things no longer matter to Russ; only now was he able to be his true, full self.

We ended up having dinner and drinks with that couple every night we spent in Eze. I'm ashamed to admit that I've forgotten their names, but if I were to call them Bill and Kay or Francesca and Louis or even by their real names, it would not change the joy I felt at getting to make brand-new friends alongside my husband in a way we'd stopped doing fairly early into our marriage.

Our new friends were more than able to afford our hotel and meals, yet Russ insisted on treating them every night. At first, they balked—they were kind and generous people—but eventually, Russ leaned forward, laid his hand on the arm of the other man, and said, without drama but with utter sincerity, "Truly, it's my treat. I don't have many treats left to give."

And so it was that we found ourselves telling our situation to our new friends, and upon our parting, they embraced us with tears running down their faces, saying how overwhelmed and happy they were to have gotten to spend this special time with us. I would end up sending them a card to notify them after Russ had died, and receiving in response a beautiful note about the special memories they would always have of us and the trip.

Only now, looking back from this distance, do I realize that not remembering their names is likely a trauma response—as present as I was trying to be for Russ, I was at times walking around in a fog. I'd only just gotten through my own cancer; my mother was deteriorating with dementia; my second husband was dying; somewhere, back in the United States, Michael had come to some kind of understanding with Russ, and yet we were in a limbo of sadness and confusion. Yes, we had wanted to be together, but not like this. Not at the cost of Russ's life. My mind flitted like a fruit fly, unable to land on anything for long. I thought of our sons, back at home. I thought of Doug and Grace/Lindsay and Tom/Mike and Caroline, our kind and openhearted new friends, friends who have disappeared now into the void of time and memory lapses but remain etched in my mind. (I find myself hoping that, somehow, they will read this someday and know how much pleasure they helped bring to Russ, rendering our days in Eze more normalized, more social, the perfect last hurrah we'd hoped for. *Thank you*, I would tell them. *Thank you*.)

Things fall apart slowly at first, and then, all at once. Oh God, so all at once. You can blink, take a breath, turn your head, and everything is different.

We had been home from Europe for a mere two weeks when Russ entered hospice care. How was it even possible? He'd been—gruelingly, but successfully—climbing the Spanish Freaking Steps only weeks prior. Now, it was July.

We sat, shell-shocked, as we met with hospice to form a plan. In the very first visit, Russ said to our hospice nurse, "Let's get one thing straight. My older son's birthday is August 10, and I need to be alive on August 10. I promised him I would be here and I'm not going to let my son down."

Kindly, the nurse nodded at him, her solemn expression showing how seriously she took his words.

But as I escorted her out, she turned to me and said in a low voice, "Maryellen, I don't know if we're going to be able to keep that promise."

Things fall apart...

By August 1, a hospital bed had been delivered and set up downstairs. If you've had the misfortune of having one of these beds in your home, you know how atrociously unattractive and bleak they are. I did everything I could to make the environment otherwise comforting and nice for Russ—hanging his favorite artwork within sight of the bed, decorating the area with family photos, making sure the bed was made up with the most comfortable linens and duvet—but there was nothing else for it: This was a bed in which people lay down to die.

Once this bed became *your* bed, you would never have another.

The thing about tragedy is that you are never exempt from the logistics. The time had come to call family and friends, to invite those who could to come and say goodbye. And into our home the people poured, exchanging stories with Russ at first and then, once he had grown too weak to do much talking, doing all the storytelling about their shared pasts themselves. Sharon and Terry came, of course; my twice-mother-in-law wept at Russ's bedside, but his father, ever formal, repressed, and inaccessible, left without shedding a single tear.

Witnessing this, I found myself enraged. Truth be told, even writing about it now, my heart has started racing. How different Russ's entire life—and *death*—would have been if only his father could have shown him love and affection. How different our entire marriage would have been . . . or perhaps Russ would not have still been a bachelor in his forties, would have long before found a true love of his own, had children with her, had years of joy instead of the empty and lonely life he'd often said he led prior to becoming Brett and Colton's father. I want to grant Terry grace and make excuses for him—clearly, he was not shown how to love at a young age either, and as epigenetics have now shown us, trauma literally changes our DNA so that we become a kind of science experiment whose emotional lives are dictated by a string of ancestors we may never even have met.

And yet. Yet Russ had defied those odds. He'd become a father so different from the father his had been. He'd figured out how to show love. And though he'd had no biological children whose genes could be changed by his having learned this fundamental human task of loving others, the mark he'd made on Brett and Colton would pass his care on to future generations of our family. Rather than allowing his father to break him, Russ had saved our sons in their hours of greatest need, after Steve's death. He had broken the chain.

In gratitude, I wept. Out of love, I wept.

Each day, a new hospice nurse would come to our home to check on Russ. Even up to a week before his death, I was still doing most of his homecare, bathing him and changing his diapers. But by August 6, Russ had deteriorated too much for me to manage all of this alone anymore. He was in pain, and his new nurse, a lovely man named Rick, started him on morphine so that his pain would be manageable.

Sure enough, at the relief of his intense discomfort, Russ fell into a deep and peaceful sleep. But Rick stayed on, eating dinner with the group that had come that day to say their goodbyes. He expressed how lucky he felt to be with such a wonderful family, and something in my heart began to thaw further. Deep within me, I found full forgiveness for the mistakes Russ and I had made, and instead saw us through Rick's eyes: Yes. Yes. We were a wonderful family. We were lucky. We were blessed.

Everyone on our hospice team knew about Russ's desire to make it to August 10. Just before he left that night, Rick took my hands and looked into my eyes.

"The end is near now, Maryellen," he said, gently but firmly. "Whatever you need to do regarding Brett's birthday, I advise you do it soon."

Then, all at once . . .

I knew Russ had written a card out to Brett—back when he was still able to sit, to write, merely a week or so prior. And so, to a string of many Hard Things poor Brett had already been through, I added another—one of the hardest things I've ever done: I went to my ten-year-old child and told him, "Honey, Dad needs to celebrate your birthday today."

Brett looked at me, confused. "But, Mom, he's asleep."

I wiped tears from my eyes. "He'll know you're there, sweetie. Let's just go in and do what we can."

I watched as my young man, so responsible for too many adult things before his time, bravely went and sat on the edge of Russ's bed. Because Russ was asleep, I handed Brett the card he had written, and I narrated aloud what was happening, like one might when raising a toddler—"Oh, now Brett is here to celebrate his birthday! Look, Russ, Brett is opening your card!"

I watched as Brett read the words his father had written, and then withdrew eleven one-hundred-dollar bills, one for each of his eleven years. Brett handed me the money, numbly, with no idea what to do with such a sum, but held on to the card in which his father had written how proud he was of him and how much he loved him. He had not been saying much as he sat at Russ's bedside, but finally he said, in a louder voice than he would usually use, "Thank you for making it to my birthday. I love you, Dad."

And at the sound of his son's voice, from his comatose state—a state from which he had not moved in days—Russ miraculously rose to a fully seated position, put his arms around Brett, and embraced him.

Russ spoke no words, and just as soon as he'd sprung up, he lay back down.

THE ROAD TO YESTERDAY

The next morning, when Rick showed up for his second day of work, I answered the door in tears. Rick immediately pulled me into a long, tight hug, tears in his own eyes too.

My second husband—a complicated, flawed, heroic, fun, and beautiful man, a wonderful father, and one of the truest friends of my life—had died during the night.

CHAPTER 9
THE DOG DAYS ARE (ALMOST) OVER

How do we metabolize accumulated losses that happen over multiple seasons of our lives, the hard times flying like a banner of grief over all the everyday experiences that come after? Is it an issue of simply "moving on," or of getting up each morning and moving *through*, knowing that moving *beyond* is one of so many misconceptions regarding loss?

These questions ran beneath my days like a steady pulse, a river of thought; all these years later, they still do. The beauty of love is matched by the brutality of grief. Perhaps life is always like this: The dinners and the conversations and the concerts and the laughter and the lovemaking is a mirror of all those same experiences that have come before—in another season, another decade, another life.

Russ died in August, at the height of summer, when Southern California days mean full sun on baking asphalt, cars snarled in traffic on freeways shimmering in the heat, the bright pop of bougainvillea blooms filling the air with a sweet and hopeful fragrance, and warm nights with an occasional soft and easy wind. That summer, for me, was a strange emotional cocktail: a bit of survivor's guilt, a bit of shock, a bit of relief that

Russ was no longer suffering, a bit of hope for the future, as he'd given Michael and me his blessing to move forward together before his death. What was next? I felt exhausted, saturated with emotion, and overwhelmed, as I knew far too well how much there was to do in the wake of someone's death.

In this case, first on my list was comforting my boys, who had lost their father. Again.

As I have always done, I rallied my people. I called Gina and told her, "It's time to come," and like the loyal best friend she had always been, she arrived on August 9, the day after Russ died, and pulled me into a long, silent hug. We needed no words; she held me, we cried together, and I wondered again how anybody navigates the world without women friends.

I knew well that loss brings out the best and the worst in people, and while it was no secret that Russ's father—now having lost *two* sons and a stepson—was not exactly a doting father, even I had underestimated this quality in him when he expressed little interest in helping with the funeral. Was it grief that made him so disinterested and disconnected? I don't know, but I found it deeply sad.

When I tried to explain this to Gina, I felt like I was eating chalk. She shook her head and said, "He's the one who's missed out, being so closed off."

It was true—Terry had never been able to take the joy in his family that he could have if he'd stopped judging, comparing, dominating. Yet, even so, I found it hard to empathize—perhaps too hard, I think now. Then, I saw only the impact of Terry on Russ, and rarely wondered what makes a man like Terry the way he is. How many rejections and judgments, and how much pain might he have faced long before losing two sons—a fate no parent should have to bear?

I couldn't ask myself this question then, and as Gina and I talked, I felt my emotions lowering deeper and deeper, past shock, past anger, and into a place of deep pain. "I'm selfishly thankful that Russ was there to father Brett and Colton when they needed it most," I told her, "but what I really wish for him—what he should have had—will never be. By the time I lost Steve, Russ should have had his own family, his own children—he should have been running Terry's company like he planned to—he was perfectly capable! I feel like he's being passed over *again*, even in death."

Gina held my fists in her hands, unfurled them, and reassured me, "If Russ were here, he wouldn't be wishing for some different life without you in it. Your sons were his sons too. His life wasn't perfect, Mare, but he wouldn't have traded Brett and Colton for anything."

I knew she was right, and yet still these thoughts plagued me and intensified my grief.

Thankfully I couldn't dwell on Terry too much, because soon the whole family would gather to be with me and the boys. I was looking forward to having a house full of people who would offer me support, kindness, and an extra hand to attend to the *busyness* that planning a funeral necessarily entailed. This part of grief felt like a worn-in glove that fit all too well, and yet it was this type of support that had gotten me through losing Steve, and I was grateful I would have it again, as strange as it felt to *need* it again. This was the cruelest game of déjà vu.

While Russ was still living, we had each confided in family members about Michael, of course including that Russ had given his blessing to the both of us to continue and deepen our relationship. I was deeply relieved that there would be no secrecy, and again thanked Russ silently for how loving and urbane he had been in his understanding. Everything was out in the open. There was literally nothing to hide, nothing to be ashamed about—he had given me that as a parting gift.

In the frenzied activity around hospice and final goodbyes, I had not lingered much on what anyone else might think about our unusual situation. I thought only of how Russ had faced his own death like a gentleman, with dignity and compassion. Between us, Michael had been a nonissue.

How strange, then, that when my family members began to arrive I abruptly felt self-conscious, like I was some modern version of Hester Prynne in *The Scarlet Letter*, walking around with an "A" painted on my chest. My parents and brothers had flown cross-country to support me as I grieved Russ, and yet here I was, in love with another man—and they all knew it.

As I gathered glasses in the kitchen for everyone, I found myself muttering under my breath, talking to Russ, "*We shouldn't have told them.*" My own words threw me . . . in our valuing of honesty between us, it had never occurred to me that perhaps Russ and I should have kept Michael to ourselves, that my family wouldn't understand. Would they think my grief false—imagine I was somehow rubbing my hands together like an evil Disney character, delighted to have my husband out of the way so I could run into my waiting lover's embrace? Were they silently condemning me as a hypocrite every time my eyes welled over for Russ?

As we poured wine and sat around the living room largely in silence, I couldn't tell the difference between the hush of shock and grief and the judgmental silence of a jury scrutinizing me. I'd been longing for my family's arrival, but now I wanted to hide from their eyes.

Looking back on this time, I understand that I was still processing my deep guilt around my failed marriage to Russ—or how I perceived it as a failure—and as an already highly sensitive person who didn't respond well to criticism, I was up in my head, spiraling, projecting feelings on my family that were, in reality, my *own* feelings. Just because Russ had not only forgiven me for Michael but also sanctioned our future relationship did not mean I'd let go of my *own* self-castigation for cheating on Russ before I'd known he was sick—for planning to leave him.

How justified I'd felt at the time! I'd been lonely, felt unloved and unseen—yes, this was all true. But Russ and I had grown so much closer in the final months of his life that now I saw my own past actions with different eyes. When I thought of the day Russ learned of his dire diagnosis—of Michael even having to be part of his consciousness, a worrying stone beneath his attempts to live life fully while he could—I cringed inwardly. My dissatisfaction with our marriage, although it had spanned years, felt small to me now in the wake of Russ's premature death. Why had I not been more patient? Why had I needed so much more than he could give? Was something wrong with me? Was it my imagination that my parents and brothers all saw me differently now? When Steve died, I'd been the tragic young widow—now, I was some kind of Black Widow, not deserving of sympathy. This complicated cocktail of emotions whirred around my brain until I felt out of place in my own home.

I can see now that I interpreted the quiet sadness of *mourning* as judgment, despite knowing that hollow sadness—that liminal space between someone's death and the ceremony of a funeral to say goodbye—all too well. It's like being suspended in midair, waiting to fall, anticipating the crash, wondering how it will feel and what the aftermath will look like. A deep sense of disquiet and despair hung over us as we, as a group, did this all over again: Came together to mourn. Planned another funeral. Comforted children who'd lost a father.

Yet because I interpreted the silence of the people around me as disapproval, I shut down and became quiet, too, reticent. If the only way I could mourn without judgment was by being alone, then I would be alone.

By the time my parents arrived, I had climbed into bed and stayed there. I had no strength to be anywhere else.

When my parents found me there in my bedroom—stunned, silent, a shell of a person—a single look passed between us, and the sobs began. They both crawled in next to me, holding me for dear life.

As a mother, I understood that the hardest moments of being a parent are watching your child in pain of any kind, so I knew this was excruciating for them. How would I feel if Brett or Colton, as adults, were in this situation? How could my parents possibly, *for the second time*, watch their only daughter go through so much pain? I could imagine them screaming, *Enough already!*

In my parents' embrace, my fear of their disapproval began to loosen. *You're being crazy*, I told myself. *Nobody is judging you!*

Or maybe they were? We are all human beings, and in truth love and judgment are not as mutually exclusive as we might wish.

Those days before the funeral were particularly fraught for David and me. He'd called my and Michael's relationship an "affair" the first time he heard about it, and this stung. Hard.

I found myself talking back to imagined indictments in my head. *Sure, if I'd left Russ and* married *Michael, then Michael would be my* husband, I ranted silently, *but because I actually did the right thing and stood by Russ's side, Michael will always be thought of as my clandestine lover.* I found myself barely able to meet David's eyes, thinking he had lost all respect for me even though he, having left an unhappy marriage himself, should have been the one I felt most understood by.

If my family noted that I was acting strangely, that I was prickly and abnormally quiet, they didn't mention it. I felt like a grenade tossed into the middle of our well-appointed living room. Again and again, I retreated to my bedroom and climbed under the covers to hide—perhaps from myself most of all.

As ever, Gina knew what to say and how to say it. I heard a soft knock and her voice on the other side of the door one day, asking if she could come in. I dragged myself up and opened the door, and we crawled into bed together.

"I know you're sad and I know this is a weird time," she said softly. "I know you've been in this position before, and I know it's totally unfair. It's all just really fucking hard."

I started to cry.

Holding my hand, she continued, "Even though you don't want to, we have to get you out of this room and out of the house. C'mon, let's go for a drive. Get some fresh air. Everyone is getting antsy."

As we prepared to make a drive to Malibu, two men from hospice were coming into and going out of the house—first with Russ's hospital bed, empty now, perhaps headed for another patient. They loaded it into a long black sedan and then brought out all the other equipment, useless now and looking utterly out of place. I began to sob at this dreadful and depressing sight—so final, so empty. I turned to David and said, "Get me out of here. Now!"

Without waiting for a response, I climbed into the front seat. Everyone else—David, Gina, Sandy, my niece Chrystn, and her girlfriend, Louisa—piled into the car too.

At least Malibu would mean a change of scenery, a change of air, a bit of time in the summer sunshine before becoming completely consumed by the memorial service.

Too bad, then, that the tension in the car was thick enough to be cut with a knife. Nobody talked as we sped along the road, each of us trapped in our own thoughts.

When we arrived at the beach, which was packed with children running back and forth between their in-progress sandcastles, watchful parents lounging under wide umbrellas, and sweaty sunbathers of all ages diving into the warm water and then out again, their hair and limbs dripping wet, everyone ran ahead, but David stayed back.

He seemed distracted and uneasy. His uncharacteristic silence indicated to me that he had something to say, but unless it was a statement of love and support, I didn't want to hear it. Couldn't he see how out of sorts I was? I needed my rock of a brother right now, not this strange reticence.

I tried to focus on the crash of the water against the sand, the dark shapes of surfers far out in the water, waiting to catch a wave, and the shifting clouds over a sandy beach on a high summer day.

David finally broke his silence. "So, uh. Michael isn't going to be at the funeral, is he?"

I don't know if I saw red, the way people often describe feeling intense anger, but I couldn't remember a time when

I had been so angry or overwhelmed. My bones, my skin, my heart—I was on fire with it. "No, he's not going to be at the funeral, David," I shot back. "How could you think I could be so cold? I thought you knew me!"

I quickly walked away before I said anything more, or anything I might regret, tears of frustration and rage and sadness and *I cannot even believe this* blurring my vision. I was right! They were all playing judge and jury, deliberating the Problem of Me behind my back, in my own home. My boys and I were in *mourning*, I was a widow for the second time in less than a decade, and yet here I was, feeling sized up and made to feel like a bad person, a bad *woman*, despite my having chosen my duty as a wife even when I'd believed it would mean forever, not nursing my husband to the precipice of death. Was my family, who had been on the other side of the country while I was tending to Russ's dying body, really sending David like some ambassador to see if I planned to make out with Michael on my husband's casket?

In my mind, David's audacious question was the last straw; I'd had enough.

I stormed over to the spot the others had staked out on the beach. They all turned to look at me, which only made the fire in my body burn brighter. I felt like screaming, but instead I crossed my arms, fumed silently, and tried to stop the tears from coming.

Everyone was lying quietly on their towels, not saying a word. The only sounds were muted conversations from nearby beachgoers, the occasional tremor of laughter, the crack of a beer being opened. I caught Gina's eye, and she gave me a knowing, tender look.

After a few minutes of silence that felt like hours, Gina stood up, dusted the sand from her legs, and said, "Right. Sandy and David, let's go for a walk."

They agreed, and as I watched them strolling down the sand, side by side and barefoot, I bent my knees, set my head on my lap, and let the tears fall.

Later, Gina told me what she said to David and Sandy. With none of the trepidation or shame I felt, she'd announced to them, "Maryellen is my best friend, and I've spent a lot of time with her and Russ, and you don't know the whole story about how it was for your sister." She relayed to them what a lonely existence marriage to Russ had been for me so much of the time. She told them that until Russ's diagnosis and the closeness we'd developed during our joint cancer journeys, I had been lonely and sad and confused from the day of my honeymoon onward.

"Maryellen didn't think her life would end up this way," she told them. "She tried as hard as anyone could to make the marriage work—I won't go into all the details, but trust me, I know how hard she tried. And listen to me, *Russ* understood how hard she tried. Not only did they come to peace, but in the end, they deeply loved each other. Russ would want Maryellen to be happy!"

Of course, I wouldn't learn until later what had been said. At the time, I sat on the sand with a hammering heart and eyes that felt like scorched holes in the earth.

By the time Gina and my brothers had returned from their walk, the fire had burned down a bit and I had composed myself. Without a word, we all picked up our towels and walked to the car.

On the drive home, the silence continued—in fact, this time it felt even more oppressive. The sun was blazing through the car windows, and I felt sweat on my neck and upper lip. We passed couples holding hands, hauling picnic baskets to the beach, navigating the skinny sidewalks lining the Pacific Coast Highway. The ocean glimmered like a promise, but a promise of what? Was I going to be judged for every move I made from now on? Would I continue to judge myself although I knew in my heart that I'd done the best I could? If Michael and I were lucky enough to make it all work out, would my family ever accept him? Would they want to meet him at all, or would we be expected to live in secret, like outcasts, even though we were perfectly free to be together?

I didn't plan to lose it, but I lost it.

"Pull over," I suddenly commanded.

David looked at me like I was kidding, or out of my mind, or maybe both. Nobody took me seriously. Nobody understood. I thought of Steve. I thought of Russ. I remembered all I was holding in my heart and holding up in my life. I was beyond the point of bearing it any longer.

"Pull over the car right now!" I screamed.

Clearly shocked, David pulled over.

With shaking hands and a trembling voice, I yelled, "How dare any one of you judge me when I'm going through this. *How dare you!* I've been lonely and scared and sad, and I've lost two husbands to tragedies, and you're going to treat me like I'm some fallen woman? This is unacceptable!"

Sandy and David, both as dumbstruck as I'd ever seen them, looked as if they might say something, or try to—but I wasn't finished, not by a long shot, and now that I'd started saying what was on my heart, what I had needed to say for so long, I couldn't stop.

Gina nodded, gently encouraging me to speak my mind.

"Really, you guys?" I continued. "A man *has needs* when he's lonely, so it's okay if he finds love, right? Is this really the double standard we're talking about right now? Would you ever in a million years act this way toward a man who had just spent months nursing his wife while he himself had cancer too? Don't even answer me—I *know* you wouldn't!"

We were all crying now, in this car on the side of the road that wound past one of the most picturesque beaches in the country and maybe even the world. But really, we were all marooned on the planet of grief, in that strange, cold, and unwelcoming landscape where there are no road signs or lights illuminating the way forward and the terrain is always changing.

Nobody spoke. Had my words even made sense to them? Did they resonate, deep down, with some inner critic inside the bodies of my family members—or did they merely think me raving mad? Traffic speeding past made our car shake as if we were in a mild earthquake.

We sat there for a long time. But we couldn't stay there forever. Russ's funeral was the next day, and there was still so much to be done. We all seemed to be out of words and out of tears. Eventually, David pulled away from the curb and we headed home, once again in silence that felt as loud as the loudest, most persistent drumbeat.

I felt exhausted, but also as if I'd shrugged a weight from my back and left it there on the side of the PCH. I felt cleansed of the need to scream, rage, and rail.

As we drove, I heard sniffling in the otherwise silent car. Whether or not they related to what I'd said, no one had rebuffed me. I remembered again how much my family loved me. They always had. They always would. Unconditionally.

When we got back to the house, we all embraced and took a deep, unified breath. We knew what we had to do next: get ready for a funeral.

A grim task, but much easier to address now that the air had been cleared.

I couldn't sleep that night, and again Gina crawled into bed with me and held my hand until I fell asleep, which I finally did around sunrise. When I woke, just as she had done the morning of Steve's funeral, she got me dressed, gave me half a Xanax, and handed me a piece of toast on a napkin.

"You've got to eat," she said gently, her kind eyes comforting me.

"I can't believe we're doing this," I said, trying to swallow the sob rising in my throat.

Gina's eyes filled with tears as she watched me, once again, force down food on the morning of my husband's funeral.

"Here we are with you putting the goddamn toast down my throat again," I muttered. I was in that numb state of having slept only an hour, if that, when the body wants to collapse but is kept upright and moving by sheer adrenaline and necessity. My face looked hollow and sad, and no amount of makeup seemed able to brighten the dark circles beneath my eyes. I wanted to crawl back under the pile of blankets on the bed and never leave.

Gina hugged me. "We'll get through this. Let's go."

THE ROAD TO YESTERDAY

That morning of the funeral, while I was trying to compose myself with Gina's help, everyone left the house to go horseback riding, a distraction for Brett and Colton. Gina and I stayed behind and lay back down in bed so I could grab a much-needed nap.

When I woke, not rested but at least partially revived, I peered out the window to find my three brothers stoically washing the cars that would take us to the funeral, the water glimmering in the sunlight, water pooling around the wheels and running down the driveway. Needless to say, nobody had asked my brothers to clean all of our cars, and I understood that they were doing it for me as a gesture of care and respect, of wanting to make everything as right as it could be. I momentarily closed my eyes, my brothers' broad shoulders, hunched a bit in heavy grief, still in my head. In that moment, I released anything I had been carrying, including the resentment I'd felt over how David had spoken about Michael. That was *my* David—out there making our cars gleam so that our funeral procession would be befitting of what Russ had meant to us all, and what we meant to one another.

And then there we were again, like a bad dream set on repeat: everyone—once again—standing gathered at the bottom of the stairs, solemn and formal in our dark attire.

Everyone, that is, except Brett, who refused the whole idea, the whole fact, of this funeral. My heart broke with the unfairness of it all; that Brett would have to lose two fathers in the span of his youth was a wound I knew could never be fully healed, no matter what joys might lie ahead for him.

I also knew that if he didn't go to the funeral, he would regret it forever. But I didn't have the energy to insist, to have a scene.

"I'll go talk to him," David said, responding to my lost look and clearly noting how worn out I was. He and Brett were close, and I also felt that David wanted to show me how sorry he was for the day before; he wanted to show me, yet again, that he was always and forever on my side. I met his eyes before he headed upstairs, trying to convey through my own eyes, *I know*.

We waited awkwardly in our funeral clothes, and then I heard a door open and there was Brett, his eyes red, dressed in a suit and barreling down the stairs as if he wanted to break them.

"I'll go," he said, his voice thick with emotion, "but I'm not wearing a tie."

I embraced him, my boy who, now more than once, had been thrown into the role of manhood too soon; I understood this small rebellion as a way of both protesting Russ's death and as a reminder of how young he truly was. I put my arm around him protectively as we exited the house.

The funeral itself went by in a blur: hymns, prayers, remembrances, sitting up and sitting down, the pastor's words, a reading from Scripture. I was so grateful to be alive, while also so desperately sad; holding these two truths at once was wildly disorienting. Through the haze of fatigue and sleeplessness, I felt like I was hallucinating, or existing somewhere outside of time, or maybe in a different time entirely. Was this Steve's funeral, or Russ's? How many times could one person be widowed? What was the nature of hope now? How would I trust in the goodness of the future? Would I be damaged, lose the ability to choose the present moment—to choose love—for fear of what might loom ahead? Was it safe to love again when funeral processions were what my love had wrought? And if I managed to find that leap of faith, if I managed not to be widowed a third time, then would it someday be Michael, numb and floating above his body as he bade goodbye to me? How could *anything* be worth this pain—either as the one left behind or the one mourned by a beloved?

I looked at Sharon's bent head; her outfit and hairstyle were perfect, but her mouth trembled as she whispered a prayer. No matter what I thought of her husband, Russ's father, this was a woman who had lost at least as much as I had, maybe more. She had buried her son, and although she had not raised Russ, she had cared for him enough that she'd steered the two of us together, trying to make for us both a family, *her* family.

I closed my eyes, held the hands of my boys, the three of us navigating loss once again, in public, and yet also as a unit of three, privately and in our own ways, both seen and unseen. *This is love*, I thought. *And this is loss, and this is life—my life—and this is just a moment, but it is also everything.* I squeezed my boys' hands as hard as I could and prayed for strength and guidance, hoping both would find me if I couldn't find them.

It was no surprise that everyone was emotionally exhausted after the funeral, and even more so after we'd all had a few glasses of wine and picked at the food. I had a macabre thought about funeral food; really, what was the point? Grief obliterated taste as well as hunger. Everything tasted like the dry toast I'd reluctantly choked down that morning.

Even from this distance, I can see myself like a pale ghost in that house; I can remember the sensation of knowing my body was moving but feeling as though I were not *inside* it, precisely, but rather as if someone else had been poured into the outlines of my body. I didn't recognize this Maryellen and didn't know what to do with her. I also still felt like I had failed somehow, especially since my outburst the day before. My own family was a bit afraid of me now, treading lightly on eggshells lest they set me off.

My adult niece, Chrystn, David's daughter, caught my eye and smiled. She approached me and held out a hand. "Let's go talk," she said, and I gratefully followed her up the stairs, happy to be out of the silent but awkward post-funeral fray.

Not so long ago, but what felt like a lifetime ago, on the one-month anniversary of 9/11, I'd attended a memorial service at a local church. I'd been endlessly watching the footage on the news that morning, and it felt like a strange relief to be sitting with grieving people rather than watching the towers fall over and over again. The buildings were standing, and then they were crumbling, again and again: dust and fire under the sunlight and blue sky. I didn't want to watch and yet I couldn't stop watching; I turned the television off, I switched it on again. Sitting in the fourth-row pew with my boys that long-ago morning—they were so young!—one on each side, I cried and cried, entirely overwhelmed. I was still in the stunned stage of grief, floating in a kind of daydream that felt more like a waking nightmare. As I sobbed and held my boys' hands, a woman rubbed my shoulder without saying a word, the warmth of her hand a momentary and welcome balm for my emotional distress.

Months later, Chrystn, who was then in college, began dating a woman, Louisa, and when Louisa saw a newspaper clipping of a photo taken on that day that was hanging in Chrystn's dorm room, she was stunned. "Why do you have that picture?" she asked. When Chrystn explained that it was *me*, her aunt, in the photo, Louisa exclaimed, "But that's my *mother* with her hand on your aunt's shoulder." Louisa had lost her father in the towers on 9/11. It is so strange how grief divides us from our loved ones, and yet connects us to others who hold us up—literally and metaphorically—in ways we never could have orchestrated or imagined on our own.

Now, Chrystn clearly recognized how deeply I needed a compassionate ear, and though only twenty-eight, she was wise beyond her years. We sat together on the bed. I poured out my feelings; she held my hand and listened.

"I feel like people just don't comprehend how things have been for me," I began.

Chrystn listened patiently.

"I don't mean to feel sorry for myself, but I've been to hell and back more than once, and I feel like . . . does that make me a bad person? Is it selfish of me to dare hope this won't be all my life entails?"

In a torrent, I told her all about the whirlwind romance with Russ and how Sharon had made the initial connection happen. It felt so freeing to talk about what the roller coaster of these last several years had been like, how full of dramatic ups and wild downs, with very little breathing room in between. And at last, I also spoke of Michael—of the easy friendship, the laughter, the effortless joy we'd felt together; of how he'd been there for me during my cancer even though I'd not spoken to him in months, had cut him off; of how I knew his love for me still burned strong.

"It's not in my nature to just lie down and disappear," I told Chrystn at last. "I'm grieving, and I know being with Michael won't make that pain disappear, just like caring for Russ and witnessing the slow horror of his decline didn't make me forget what loving Michael felt like. I loved them both—I still love Steve too! Life is more complicated than people act like it's supposed to be. I can't just empty myself out to be only the grieving widow. I *am* that, but I'm more than that too."

Chrystn looked straight at me and said, "Damn, Aunt Mare. You're a survivor, is what you are. You're doing an amazing job, and you deserve to be happy."

I felt so bonded to my wise niece in this moment. This was just what I'd needed to hear, and I immediately felt myself becoming more real again, the outlines of my body filling in, filling out, becoming a version of me that I could recognize, even if only fleetingly. In that singular moment, hope and strength—through my niece, who I knew had faced her own share of judgments from the world—had found me once more.

And then it was the three of us—me, Colton, and Brett—all over again.

After everyone had gone home, I was plunged back into a new loneliness, living in a place where I didn't have many friends. I wanted to leave sunny California for another sunny place. This was something Russ had known I wanted to do, and had fully and actively supported. In fact, we'd planned my departure together while he was still alive. He knew better than anyone else what I would need in the next chapter of my life, and part of his final gift to me had been to help me secure what parts of it he could.

Way back in 2004, I'd visited Hailey, Idaho—a town not far from the more well-known Sun Valley—for the first time. I'd felt immediately drawn to the fresh air, the mountains rising regal and sharp in the distance, the sunshine and space that made every street and every neighborhood feel clean and fresh—the very definition of a new start. "God, I'd love to live here someday," I'd said then. I didn't want to live in a city with tall buildings and big airports. It felt too precarious; these wide-open spaces in a place that had a slower pace and fewer people felt much safer.

When Russ was sick, with his knowledge and his blessing, I'd bought a home in Hailey with my own money, although I hadn't told the boys that yet.

Now, as I'd done so many times before, I sat the boys down and said, "Do you want to go to Hailey for the weekend?"

As always, the boys said yes.

Michael picked us up at the airport, and the boys were thrilled to see him. Although they didn't yet know that Michael and I were planning to be together, or that we already had a home to move into, they both had spent a lot of time with Michael over the years when Russ was working in California. Long before Michael and I had ever shared our kiss on his back deck, he had been a family friend who'd taken them fishing and been a good pal to them both.

I was older now than I had been when I'd watched my boys take such a shine to Russ after Steve's death, and my sons were older too. Colton, of course, didn't remember Steve at all; he only knew photos and stories. Russ was my sons' father, and neither Michael nor I had any delusions that he was going to just step into that role. We wouldn't have wanted that. I vowed to always honor the position Russ had in my sons' lives, and their mutual love, and I hope I have always lived up to that vow.

Still, as we ate lunch one classic Idaho summer afternoon, with sunshine and blue skies and birds singing in every tree, Brett turned to me and said, "Mom, why do we *have* to go back to California? There's nothing there for us anymore."

I put down my water glass. "Well, boys, it just so happens that I've found the perfect place for us here. If it's what we want, we can stay."

The happy relief on Brett's and Colton's faces was palpable, and I knew then I'd made the right choice. Michael beamed. The next chapter of my life—and our lives together—was beginning to take shape. Brett could start fresh in a new school where he wouldn't have to face yet more questions about a dead father.

Back in September of 2001, the thought of living alone with my sons, without a man in our home, had terrified me. After Steve's death, I'd let fear drive me—far too soon and without enough forethought—into a second marriage I wasn't ready for, with a man for whom I wasn't well suited. Because of that, I hadn't been alone since I was a girl of twenty-five.

Now a middle-aged woman, a two-time widow, a cancer survivor, a homeowner capable of standing on my own, I was no longer afraid. Michael and I would continue to live apart for some time—to allow the boys time to adjust to us as a couple, yes, but also to allow *ourselves* time to adjust and grow together too. This time, I knew that if our love was meant to be—as I suspected it was—there was no rush. This time, I was going to give that love time to blossom, knowing that I had what it took to stand alone.

So it was that now we had a place to go and a community to greet us. The only hurdle that remained was breaking the news to Sharon, as I knew that, after everything, not playing a game of hedging and avoidance was the least I owed her.

As soon as I was back in California, I braced myself and called my mother-in-law.

The minute the words "we're moving" came out of my mouth, Sharon gasped and exploded, "How dare you take my grandchildren away! They just lost their second father!"

I bristled. I had just lost my second *husband*. But rather than fire back, I took a deep breath, counted to five in my head, then asked her to come over and talk about it in person.

I sat, awaiting her arrival, both in dread and like a coiled snake ready to strike. I was in no mood to listen to her rant about me taking my sons away from California. I was going to set the record straight with her once and for all about why I *had* to get away from the place that never felt like home to me. This move was for me and my sons and no one else.

Sharon showed up about an hour later, agitated and downtrodden but with perfectly styled hair and immaculate makeup, as always. When I saw her standing in the doorway, I softened toward her, remembering my empathy for her the day of Russ's service, remembering that if I was a survivor, then Sharon and I were part of the same club, and so I decided to be fully honest.

I started by telling her how I felt like she had orchestrated the relationship with Russ at a time when I was extremely vulnerable. "I know that you meant well," I assured her. "I know you wanted to help me, you wanted to help your grandsons, and you wanted to help Russ too. But I felt pushed into it, at a time when I wasn't thinking straight."

I paused—rather dramatically, I realized—as though expecting Sharon to shout at me, to deny every insinuation. But she didn't, and again I softened further. Here we were, two veterans of the same war. Could Sharon's marriage to a man like Terry be an easy one? Had she, too, yearned for more, or were we different creatures in this way, fulfilled by radically different things? I would never know, for I understood that however much we had been through together, she would never grant me that access to her interior truths.

Instead, I said, "In the end, Sharon, I am a grown woman, and I stepped into my marriage with Russ by choice, but you know as well as I do who Russ was back then. I suspect it's part of why you wanted to help him to find a family of his own. He was so reticent. Marriage didn't just magically cure that. I was terribly lonely, and I suspect Russ was lonely too. We were just not compatible. And looking back, you and I both should have known that, given that I was so compatible with Steve, who was almost Russ's total opposite."

To my surprise, although Sharon didn't say much, she seemed to be listening, and at the mention of Steve I saw her eyes grow wet—perhaps remembering us together, as I myself so often did.

"What I need you to understand is that I don't regret marrying Russ," I said. "I thank you for trying to help us. You *did* help us, even if the situation wasn't ideal. But Russ is gone now. Steve and Russ are both gone, and I need to make my own way."

Sharon had a small smile on her face, though her eyes still looked glassy with tears she was accustomed to not letting fall.

"Funny," she said softly. "I remember Steve saying the same thing to me once, long ago."

I laughed, remembering too. "And you went and dragged him home by his ear."

We both wiped our eyes.

Sharon straightened. "I guess I can't do that with you, Maryellen, can I?"

I would like to say here that we embraced, that we came to some peace right there in that moment, but instead, Sharon gathered herself regally and left. She had, for once, not gotten her way, and I did not know whether she would ever forgive me for it.

A month later—on September 11, of all days—we moved to Idaho. But first Michael flew to California to help us relocate to what already felt like home.

I couldn't wait to be back in Idaho, to feel settled in my new life. Even Sharon had come around, though she had one request: "I just want to meet Michael myself before you go."

After all we had been through, I wouldn't even have considered denying her this wish.

And so, on the day she came to say goodbye to the boys, she met the man who would ultimately stand by my side to help me as I finished raising them from boys into men.

Many months later, she would say to me, "The minute I laid eyes on him, I knew he was the right person," and her words meant more to me than she would ever know.

On July 2, 2008, on my parents' sixtieth wedding anniversary, with both of them in attendance, Michael and I were married at our home in Hailey in an early-evening ceremony witnessed by seventy of our family and friends.

It was a magical summer day—the air as clear and crisp and the sky as blue as it had been when I first fell in love with this place that was now my home. As the song "Feels Like Home" by Chantal Kreviazuk played softly, Brett and Colton walked me to Michael. His daughters, Danielle and Julia, stood by his side.

As the priest said the words "'til death do you part," strangely, I did not feel afraid, even though my grief for old losses would never disappear. I looked into Michael's eyes—as sparkling and expansive as the blue sky above us—and said, no longer with naiveté or fear but only love and excitement for our future, "I do."

Just as we finished our vows, the crowd before us gasped. There, right alongside us, a group of deer galloped through the trees, elegant, light-footed, and strong. I watched them as they leapt—a symbol of hope—and, smiling, I locked eyes with Michael. Together, we shared in the joy of their majesty—and I knew I had finally found my forever place, with this man beside me.

EPILOGUE
BECAUSE YOU BELIEVED IN ME

And suddenly, it was June 17, 2022, and there I was, the mother of the groom.

Brett was to be wed the next day to the love of his life, Jessica, at the Pronghorn Resort in Bend, Oregon. With Michael by my side, as he had now been for fourteen years, and Colton and his own beautiful girlfriend, Grete, in attendance, we prepared to watch Brett—one scant year older than I was when I first met his father—and Jess commit their lives to one another.

How could it even be true that I was now a woman in later middle age, and had been with Michael for longer than those precious years with Steve that I for so long believed would singly define my life forever? How could my brave boy—who had once hung signs on our front door to welcome home a father who would never return, who had granted Russ's dying wish to survive to watch him turn eleven—now be a grown man, strong and kind and as in love as his father and I had once been?

How fast it all goes.

The elegant Pronghorn Resort, heavy on stone and dark wood, sleek yet somehow deeply homey and comfortable, was magnificent—but torrential rain was pouring down outside. Brett (now an accountant) and Jess (an attorney) had decided on a very small wedding—ten guests only—to take place in Jess's parents' suite at the resort. Though I'd thought that choice a bit unconventional, especially considering the natural splendor of the setting, I now found myself abruptly relieved: An outdoor wedding would have been a disaster in this storm.

Still, though we would be safe and dry inside, something nagged at me. Despite how thrilled I was for Brett and Jess, there was a feeling of discomfort I couldn't shake.

I was blessed to be that rare breed of mother-in-law who knows that if she went searching the world for the perfect mate for her son, she would not find anyone better. The woman he'd chosen way back at the tender age of eighteen as a freshman at Seattle University was his match in every way. While young, they'd both simply *known* from the first, and they adored each other with both the giddy thrill of young love and, having already been together for eight years, the deep familiarity and intimacy that comes with time. They were, along with being in love, absolute best buds. I could not have wanted anything more for my son—or, for that matter, myself.

And yet I was restless, anxious.

I'd arrived in Bend with two gigantic coolers full of flowers after learning the week before that Brett and Jess hadn't made any plans in that area. They didn't seem to care about anything except getting married, and as pure and beautiful as that was, I'd insisted to Jess, "Sweetie, you have to have a bouquet." With her permission, I'd brought enough flowers to decorate her parents' entire suite.

There, the Issue of the Flowers was taken care of—check. But some low vibration still hummed under my skin, electric as the storm outdoors.

In another unconventional move, Brett and Jess were forgoing a traditional "rehearsal dinner." Given the intimate size of their wedding (comprised mostly of immediate family anyway), they'd decided to each have a quieter night with their own families of origin the night before the big event.

So, while Jess and her parents dined elsewhere, Michael, Colton, Grete, and I took Brett for a meal in downtown Bend. The food, atmosphere, and service were all so wonderful and the energy at the table was so happy and celebratory at dinner that my anxiety eased, the joy of being with my beautiful brood infectious enough that I was caught up in toasting, in the kind of familial conversations where everyone finishes one another's sentences and the laughter flows like wine. I sat content and stunned in my knowledge that if I had been able to do the choosing myself, I could not have handpicked two more perfect women for my sons.

Still, the rain poured. After dinner, walking to our car, we grew soaked. I drove carefully. Tomorrow's forecast also called for rain.

Colton, perhaps intuiting some dark undertow in my mood, said confidently to me, "Dad's definitely going to send us some kind of sign on Brett's wedding day—let's look for it."

I smiled—over the years, our family had acclimated to infrequent but unmistakable signs of Steve's continued presence in our lives. And suddenly, as we rounded a curve, I saw a sight so stunning that I stopped the car abruptly. As though we'd driven onto the set of an entirely different movie, the rain halted completely and the sun appeared as a low but vibrant ball in the sky, casting hues of orange, pink, and purple—perhaps the most beautiful sunset I'd ever seen in all my travels.

As we sat, the engine idling, each staring at the sky agog, Colton tapped my shoulder and said, "Mom. There's our sign."

My eyes brimmed with tears. It was all I could do not to wave at the sun as though greeting Steve himself. We could not have asked for a more spectacular moment, for more of a sign of the occasion's rightness and joy. Something in my anxious heart unfurled again, a flower opening—or maybe a fist unclenching.

If only I had let that sign serve as my guiding force that everything was going to be all right, that there was nothing I needed to somehow "fix." If only.

I did not drive to Bend, Oregon, with the intention of all but spoiling my son's wedding. It had been more than twenty years since Steve's death by this point, and although Michael, my sons, and I still spoke of him often, my life with Michael was such a dream come true that perhaps I believed myself "healed." In retrospect, just as I should have trusted Brett to know his own mind in terms of the type of wedding he and his love wanted, so I should have looked to the example of my son to understand that grief sometimes catches up to us when we least expect it, when we have finally stopped holding our breath and waiting for another shoe to fall—and if we don't recognize it and ask for help, it can nearly undo us.

The short version of Brett and Jess's love story goes like this: As I said, they'd met in their freshman year of college, had been virtually inseparable ever since, and now here they were, about to wed their first and only true loves. The longer story—as is true for all real-life stories—entailed some twists, some turns, some hair-raising frights, and some painful losses along the way.

Though Brett was never anything resembling a "problem child," he has always been of a beautifully sensitive disposition, an empath like his father. During his freshman year at Seattle U, like many freshmen overcome with their new degrees of freedom, he spent rather a lot of his time skipping classes and smoking pot with his two roommates, with whom he got along famously.

One terrible day, Brett came home to find that one of his two roommates, who was trans and struggling with gender identity and societal acceptance, had taken a handful of pills in a suicide attempt. Brett was the one to take them to the hospital—where, thankfully, their life was saved—and understandably, he was deeply shaken by the experience. Still reeling from the fear of it all, he and his other roommate were home the next night, shell-shocked and quiet, when that roommate abruptly had a seizure and it fell upon Brett to get help for her as well. Again, thank God, her life was saved, and neither of his roommates had their entire futures cut short on those two terrible days. Still, imagine Brett's state of mind when—on the third day—his beautiful and beloved Jess came to him, overcome with emotion, and broke the news to him that, due to circumstances beyond her control, she had to leave Seattle U and transfer to Portland State.

Both Brett and Jess were devastated, and too young and financially dependent upon their parents to know what to do about their impending separation. So, unbeknownst to me, my eldest son reached a near breaking point of stress and the fear of losing everyone he loved.

I was driving in a car with Michael and Colton when a text pinged my phone. As Michael drove, unaware of what I was reading, I looked down at a text from my son that read simply: *I'm done.*

My own confused text back: *With what?*

Brett's text: *With everything.*

I was no stranger to the way a life can change in less than a minute, but even with all I had experienced in my life, I had never known the kind of fear that rose up in my body in that moment, filling me like lava. Tears spilled from my eyes as I stared out the car window, desperate not to terrify Colton, to hide my distress. Frantically, I texted Brett back: *Please get to the airport immediately. I will get you the first flight home.*

Thankfully, he agreed, and my son who had already survived so much came home to Idaho for the following month.

During that month, he willingly went to therapy three times per week and saw a wonderful woman, Tami, who he still insists "saved my life." It was she who helped him to understand that he had never actually dealt with his grief over 9/11 and the loss of not only his father but also his childhood, his innocence. From the age of six, he'd spent his youth believing that now that he was "the man of the house" it was up to him to take care of his mom and his little brother. Then he'd bonded with Russ, only to lose him, too, before he was even a teenager. At eighteen, a dozen years after the losses of his life began accumulating, he had to go through his entire grieving process—especially for Steve—anew.

Courageously, Brett did the work he needed to do, until he no longer felt untethered from life or a risk to himself, fighting to process his long-buried emotions.

Once he stabilized enough that we were able to discuss his return to college, he asked me, "Mom, what do I do about Jess? I love her."

I said the only thing that came to my head: "Do you want to go to Portland too?"

Brett looked at me, surprised. "You'd let me just change schools?"

Maybe there are those out there who have not known the kinds of losses that make something like precisely which college their children attend relatively meaningless in the scheme of things. To any such people I can only say, *Please know how lucky you are, and how quickly such fortune can turn.* In my case, I told my son the truth: "The only thing that has ever mattered to me is that my sons are happy and safe."

Brett transferred to Portland State, where he and Jess immediately became inseparable again and both went on to become successful young adults.

And now here I was, at my son's wedding. The son I could have lost—a loss that, amongst all my losses, would have been by far the most devastating of all. I had been spared that grief, and here we were at a swanky resort in a natural paradise, and I was concerned about . . . flowers? Rain?

Freud is known to have said, *Sometimes a cat is just a cat.*

He said this precisely because, so many other times, things are *not* as they seem.

Somewhere in this vast universe, maybe there is a story in which our flawed, messy, endlessly hopeful heroine, Maryellen, goes back to her hotel room after viewing a beautiful sunset with her wonderful family and falls asleep peacefully in the arms of her husband, Michael. Maybe that version of Maryellen wakes up the day of the wedding refreshed and happy, unconcerned that the rain has started pouring down again, and has a relaxing morning before the Big Event. Maybe in that alternate version of the story, Maryellen later listens joyfully, eyes brimming with tears and joy, as toasts are made to the newlyweds. In her happiness, maybe she even drinks a bit too much champagne and stands to make a toast herself, pouring out her heart about how proud she is of not just her son but also his new wife—of their careers, their intelligence, but most of all their good and true hearts. See her there, raising her glass, saying, *May your marriage be as beautiful and full of love as the one I had with your father, may he rest in peace, and the one I am lucky enough to have again now with this man beside me, Michael.* With a lump in her throat, she may gush momentarily, *I never believed lightning could strike twice in such a beautiful way but may it—for you—strike only once and last a lifetime.* Maybe, when she is finished speaking, there is not a dry eye in the room, and Brett and Jess come forward and hug her, and someone snaps a photo, and there it is—see it?—framed on the mantelpiece as I tell this story.

Somewhere, somehow, there is a version of this story where things turn out as they should have, before the ghosts descended and had their way with me.

But this is not that story. And so, here is what happened instead:

After the lovely family dinner, the wine, the sudden astonishing sunset, I could not sit still. Yes, I had brought two coolers full of flowers, but what about *everything else* I believed an occasion as monumental as my son's wedding required?

I lay awake tossing and turning, making mental lists in my head of all that "had to" be done—not only decorating

Jess's parents' suite but also Brett and Jess's favorite restaurant, where the dinner reception would be held after the ceremony. Knowing already that I intended to do this (I had not exactly been quiet with my opinions), Jess had requested pink for the restaurant, and so I had rented every conceivable pink thing in the state of Idaho: pink tablecloths, napkins, candles, yet more flowers. While I was at it, I'd procured finer silverware than the restaurant would normally use and brought that along too. Still, as I pictured the spaces in my mind, I remained unsatisfied.

By early morning, I was already up and dressed and had enlisted Grete to help me with an emergency Target run. She and I raced through Target and other nearby stores, attempting to satisfy my manic need to make Jess's parents' suite into the kind of magical wonderland I'd envisioned. We bought white lights and candles; we procured twelve identical gold frames for the photos of Brett and Jess, at every stage of their relationship, that I'd brought from home. We dragged my portable flower-shop-in-coolers into the suite and strewed petals on the carpet like a path leading to the corner where Brett and Jess would take their vows.

While Grete willingly and in good spirit helped me, it was all me driving the show, and although Jess's parents generously indulged me and thanked me profusely for my frenzied labors, I was neither contented nor finished. Off I raced to the reception venue, leaving pink clouds of dust in my wake, jumping through yet more hoops no one had actually *asked* of me.

At the time, all I could have offered by way of explanation for my frantic interceding would have been that a wedding "should" have all these things—that they were *necessary*, that if no one else had taken care of them it was up to me to do so, and that getting married in a bare hotel suite was somehow all wrong. I came from a lineage of highly traditional romance and wooing. I'd married two consecutive men whose courtships had consisted of spectacular gestures—gestures Steve had never stopped making—and somewhere inside me I still equated love, marriage, commitment, and maybe even hope and happiness themselves with a version of romance from a brochure for a trip to Italy, with a Hallmark card or bridal magazine. I did not trust my son and the woman who had been at his side for eight years to know their own minds. And yes... yes, there was that part, the part of me that still believed things needed to look a certain way to be *right*.

But now, from this distance, having spent more than a bit of time deconstructing my actions, I understand that it was more than that.

Like Brett at eighteen, since Steve's death my life had been moving from crisis to crisis, man to man, state to state, hospital to hospital, for so long that I had never slowed down enough to allow myself time to grieve. And now, arriving at the end point of a certain era of motherhood and family—my eldest son getting married—something inside of me flew off its hinges.

I adored Michael and had my sons to consider, and so of course my own meltdown looked very different than that of an eighteen-year-old college boy texting his mother, *I'm done*. Instead, it manifested as a need to control every aspect of the environment, as though by making everything look exactly right I could miraculously erase all the pain and losses that had brought us, collectively, to this point. I could not acknowledge the grief contained inside such a beautiful day, and so I believed, somehow, that tea lights and rose petals could save us.

I should have stepped back and just showed up. Instead, I ended up sick with exhaustion. Not merely *tired*, but the kind of superhuman exhaustion that had gripped me in the days following Steve's death, the days when I could not rise from bed.

When I woke the morning of the wedding, after a scant few hours of sleep, I was already in a panic attack—heart hammering, arms numb, breath coming too fast. Despite Michael usually being my talisman, he was utterly unable to comfort me, and I found myself calling David to talk me down (as he always has—as he still does).

"Mare," my brother said calmly, "do you think any of this is just . . . you know, because your son is getting married, and his father isn't there to see it?"

The truth of this thudded like a gong in my chest, but instead of slowing my racing heart, the gong kept ringing.

Steve. Russ. Breast cancer not once but twice. The supposedly "simple" appendectomy I'd needed a decade earlier, which had ended with me throwing a blood clot through my heart and lung and almost dying (poor Michael, about to enter the room to take me home, instead overheard the doctor frantically telling me what was happening as they rushed me to get a scan, and found himself on his knees, praying to God not to take me yet). The time, not long after, in the summer of 2015, when Colton, swinging his legs, accidentally caused the split-rail fence I was sitting on to sway and send me careening backward and the top of my spleen hit a rock (at the hospital, the doctor solemnly told us that if the rock had hit literally one quarter-inch closer to my spine I would have been paralyzed for life).

Maybe, *maybe*, if it had only been my own emergencies, I could have borne up, but the very next year Michael needed open-heart surgery and this time I was the one on my knees, begging God not to take yet another husband from me. Although Michael had, of course, lived—was, five years later, still here right beside me—I lived in the perpetual PTSD of waiting for another storm to roll through and take us all: another building to fall, tumor to grow, heart to stop, plane to plummet from the sky. When would it ever stop feeling so unsafe to *be alive*; when would I stop living from catastrophe to catastrophe even in my greatest moments of joy; when would I stop fearing, at every turn, that someone I loved would turn up dead?

By the time of Brett and Jess's actual ceremony, I was so physically and emotionally exhausted that I could barely stand. Jess looked lovely in her simple, off-the-shoulder white linen dress and—ever irreverent—the offbeat pair of orange heels I'd bought her years prior. I heard my son saying, as part of his moving vows to his new wife, "There are a lot of things I have accomplished only because you believed in me," and while I felt my own cheeks moisten with tears of love, I also felt a million miles away, hovering outside my body, maybe outside Oregon altogether.

Though the rain hammered outside throughout the wedding ceremony, when we moved outdoors to take photos not a drop fell from the sky and the sun shone bright. Steve again—*Steve here; Steve long gone*. Part of me felt dead and buried with him. *Stay*, I commanded myself. *Stay, stay*. But farther and farther away I floated, some hot coil of life inside me snuffing out even as I continued to breathe.

At the tiny reception dinner, I could not even take a sip of water, let alone champagne. I could not swallow food. Before the toasts had even taken place, Michael, who had been concerned about me since that morning, finally said, "I've got to get you out of here." He had to help me walk out of my son's wedding reception.

Back in our hotel room, I sobbed as Michael tried to urge me to go to the ER. But even crying seemed too much, and I soon found myself lying straight and flat as a mummy on our strange bed. Although I was usually a stomach sleeper, I couldn't move from my corpse-like position, small and still.

I silently prayed to God that I would wake up in the morning, but in my state of mind it struck me as unlikely. *It's okay if I don't*, I told my frozen body and brain. *It's okay, because I saw my son get married.*

And mixed in with it all was my fury at myself, the horrible crush of regret. I'll never be able to take it back. Who leaves their son's wedding dinner before they can even give a toast? Perhaps surprisingly, I have few regrets in my life—but this one I knew I would carry to the grave.

I also know, a year later, that I need to let it go. Sometimes, the body can only bear up under so much. Sometimes, our love, our grief, our best intentions come out sideways. Sometimes, there is a reckoning with trauma in the middle of something blindingly beautiful, perhaps even because of the blinding beauty. Even amidst the happiest of endings, grief doesn't disappear. My story has had an almost unfeasibly happy ending, and yet it has also contained so much grief that sometimes flattens me, literally, on my back.

"Sometimes," the writer Emily Rapp, who lost one young child and is raising another, told me, "when I'm at a children's birthday party and I see all the kids running around, shrieking with glee, their strong bodies so alive and sure, my daughter's among them, I find myself crying with the beauty of it all, because the beauty is the sadness too. They're inextricable."

To this I can only add: Yes.

It is 2023, and Brett has been married for a year now; next year, Michael and I will celebrate our fifteenth wedding anniversary. Recently I found myself wondering why—here, at the close—I found it necessary to tell the story of my regrets on Brett's wedding day... interrogating why, when a memoir is by its very nature a "curated" thing that cannot possibly encompass every detail of more than half a century of life, I didn't just say, *Brett and Jess got married in June of 2022, exchanging beautiful vows*, and consider myself done with it.

As I have talked to family and friends about embarking on this writing project, I have repeatedly told them that I was driven to write a story of survival and triumph, of the saving power of love—that I hoped to inspire other women, other people who have lived through tragedies either global or intimately personal, to believe that their lives are not over, that they can survive the pain, that they can go on to be happy and lead beautiful lives, and that those lost are never really gone. Here, I can say unequivocally that I still believe every one of those things and that they have been my guiding principles in telling my story; above all else, my desire is to shine a light in the darkness for others.

What I didn't quite understand until the story was *written*, though, was that there can be no story of "survival" without a story that takes us to the very shores of the underworld, our hand outstretched to the ferryman—that stranger with no face who feels all too familiar and who seems to know our names too well—who has carted those we love away. What I did not quite understand, here in my gloriously happy third marriage, with my grown and healthy sons, is that the same elements that constitute "inspiration" almost invariably interact alchemically with moments of despair. We are—the vast, worldwide club of those who have lost too much—not merely survivors in some facile sense where the clouds have now parted and the sun shines down eternal on our happy-ever-after story. Rather, as William Faulkner wrote, "The past is never dead. It's not even past."

There is no story of overcoming without the mountain having once seemed too large to ever possibly scale. There is no story of how to reach the mountaintop without it always being necessary, inevitable, to go back down.

We survivors gather together on the top, the sun warming our faces despite the fierce breeze that reigns in high places, and we eat our snacks, drink our water, marvel at the view, take photographs of a moment that is always, by its very nature, fleeting.

So it is when two people—both married twice before—come together to live out the third act of their lives, as Michael and I did at our own wedding in 2008. Though we married in July, due to logistics and parenting and other obligations we were not able to take our honeymoon until September—coincidentally, over 9/11. We didn't go far, only to Montana for a bit of fabulous glamping, both Michael and I still vaguely stunned by the bliss of finding ourselves together when at one point we had vowed to never speak again.

So it was that on the seven-year anniversary of Steve's death, Michael and I found ourselves out for a long walk along a river, talking easily and with total trust, Michael being the man he is, about that fateful day seven years prior that had changed my life forever.

Had Steve not been killed that day in a terrible act of violence, I have absolutely not one doubt in the world that we would still be together and in love today, just as my father and my mother lived in love to the very end.

Yet here I was with my third husband, whom I loved (love) so fiercely that it was no longer quite possible to "wish for" a life in which he and I had never met at all, in which I would not have been married to Russ or lived in Idaho, in which I had never felt the shocked jolt of recognition the first time I saw Michael's blue eyes. I live with that complex truth: that the version of my life in which Steve never died, in which he and I are married still, would be characterized by a more innocent, less complicated, happiness. I would not likely be writing a memoir at all, as what would I have to tell? *I met a man and he was the love of my life, we married before I was even thirty, had two amazing sons, and lived happily ever after until we both died, peacefully, of old age?*

Sometimes, I can see that version of myself, as if on the other side of a glass. Sometimes I envy her and wonder what it would be like to be her still.

But most of the time, I don't.

As Michael and I sat by the river that day, talking about the loss of my first husband, a bald eagle suddenly swooped down in front of us, close enough to touch. And because the world is nothing if not surprising, it was my new husband who broke down crying and said, "Oh my God, that was so powerful! I feel such a connection to Steve right now, like he's really here."

And I remembered—again and again and again—why I loved this man as I did.

From that point on, bald eagles began appearing at significant family moments. "*The* bald eagle," we all came to say, though of course it is not likely they were all the precise same bird, given they have appeared to us in various states over many years. On the kids' birthdays; on a family river trip. It is a given in our family that *the bald eagle*—whether always the same or a dozen different eagles—is Steve watching over us.

If this makes me sound a little unhinged or a little too woo-woo for some, I can only say that when you have lived a life like mine, whether anyone believes that your first husband watches over your family in the body of an eagle is not one of your foremost concerns. When you have led a life like mine—and maybe like yours?—you take meaning and solace and connection when it is offered and hold it close like a diamond in your hand, and if someone else who wasn't there and never saw its shine wants to tell you it is merely a shiny rock... well, your body knows the truth.

My life with Michael has been built on a foundation of belief that Steve remains with us, a part of our family—even if only from afar and not in a way we fully understand. It takes a special kind of man—as Michael is—to not only embrace that but also to live secure in the knowledge that although the woman he is married to will never stop loving another man who is long gone, he himself is loved absolutely. While some husbands might take that as a threat, mine knows my heart enough to not interpret it that way.

Michael was married twice before, both marriages ending in divorce. When I met him, he was already retired from his law practice, living in Victor, Idaho, and under the impression that this would be the rest of his life going forward: his ranch, fishing trips, nature, peace. Not having been blessed with an earlier marriage as happy as mine was with Steve, he had concluded that marriage was not for him and that he would never embark on it again.

Then, suddenly, here he was, married to a two-time widow, fathering two boys. Although Brett was already becoming a teen with his own life, young Colton had weathered two losses he barely understood. Michael, who had been considering a return to law, ended up deferring that so that he could be singularly present until Colton left for college. He wanted to be at every soccer game and practice, to take family road trips, to be there to help with homework. Michael also taught Colton the art of fly-fishing—which, to this day, is Colton's greatest passion. Their fishing trips have included Russia, the Bahamas, Belize, Turks and Caicos, and every western state that has a river in it. Both Colton and I have always recognized and appreciated how important it was to Michael that Colton grow up with an unwavering father figure, and I believe with all my heart that it has influenced greatly the young man Colton has become.

One might think that, given how happy I was with both men, Michael must remind me a lot of Steve—but actually, it's not the case. Rather, if Michael reminds me of anyone, it's my father. I have been extraordinarily lucky in this often-brutal world that so many of the men in my life have been soft-spoken and gentle, and Michael is one of them—in possession of a huge heart, kind to everyone, filled with empathy. Now that he has gone back to law, I catch snippets of conversation sometimes between him and his clients—mainly women facing divorce and often custody battles—and I hear the way he talks to them, even at night, and how present and reassuring he is. He makes me proud, every day, to be his wife.

When Michael and I got married, each carrying our sacks of trauma on our backs in different ways, we said to each other, "The day the laughter stops it's time to just go our separate ways—no dragging it out." But it's been fifteen years and we're still laughing. Through every hard time, he's been my most stalwart advocate, and although I have been through more than enough to know I can stand on my own, I also know without question that Michael will take care of me as long as he draws breath. So many of my amazing women friends have gone through rough times during which their husbands have seemed barely present, and although Russ and I came to a deep friendship and love by the end, I know what it is to feel lonely and alone inside a marital union—so I've never taken Michael for granted or stopped appreciating the fact that he is my biggest supporter.

Marriage is *work*. Some people find this an unromantic view, but here in my third marriage, I can say with certainty that it's true. I have worked on being a better communicator with Michael than I was with Russ. My brothers and I, raised in a different era, weren't taught to be good communicators, however loving our parents were. As was viewed as polite and dignified at the time, we grew up hiding things, stuffing them down inside, rather than bringing our emotions to the surface. It took us all many years to learn that only through talking honestly can things truly be healed and turned around—but we did all eventually get there. I became even more grateful for this evolution in our sibling dynamics when we lost Scott last year, at the age of seventy, to Parkinson's disease. How many things we all might never have expressed to each other, but thankfully did. One is never too old to change and grow.

I'm also grateful to have learned this kind of mode of intimate communication with my two dearest and best (almost lifelong now) friends, Gina and Anne. They have both been through absolutely *everything* with me, and they're the ones who taught me that no part of me was unacceptable or needed to be silenced. I have always trusted them both explicitly with my thoughts and secrets. Just as was the case on 9/11, so today I still know that if I call on them, they will move mountains to be there for me. Although they live far away, there has never been any distance between our hearts.

Meanwhile, here in Idaho, Michael and I live a life of simple pleasures, surrounded by natural splendor. We enjoy going on hikes and to the movies together. Like my mother before me, when my husband comes home, I love having the table set and the candles lit and serving him a nice dinner—and like my father, Michael never fails to compliment me and thank me for my efforts. He expresses often that he loves coming home, whether just from work or an errand, and especially when he goes on fishing trips a couple times a year. "In my other marriages," he's said, "I was going on trips to get *away* from the marriage, but with you I look forward to coming home the whole time."

Once upon a time, in my darkest hours with Russ, I believed I would never again have that kind of mutual appreciation and glory in the small things, the safety and warmth of hearth and home. But life offers no guarantees aside from change, and here I am with that dream come true. When you have both been married before, as Michael and I say often, "It feels nice to get it right."

Michael is now seventy-two years old. Growing older is both the height of good fortune and also no picnic. He has aches and pains, a bad back. Even as I tell this story, I am awaiting news about a leak in one of my reconstructed breasts. After what we've both been through with our health, I would be lying if I didn't admit that we feel an acute awareness that our precarious health could turn on a dime. And yet—even though our energy isn't the same as those young people on Michael's old back deck who shared a forbidden kiss, even though we don't look the same as we once did—I still love the hell out of him and know I always will.

Sometimes Michael teases me, "I'll probably go first, and you'll get swiped up right away." At this, I just smile. For a woman who once had no idea how to live without a man, my ideas have changed. As it turns out, despite any losses I've suffered, I've also been so fulfilled in my marriages that if I am handed a chapter of life without Michael, I can't envision wanting another romantic partner. My sons, the fabulous strong and loving women in their lives, and hopefully someday my grandchildren, will be more than enough for me.

Every single year, on birthdays, Christmas, and anniversaries, Michael writes me a letter (*I know! Where did I find this amazing man?*); he has done so since our first year together. This last Christmas, he gathered all the letters together in a binder. When he presented it to me, his new letter read, *If this were my last Christmas, I would die a happy man.*

As I looked up from the binder and gazed with wonder and love on my husband, a kind of split screen opened inside my mind, as so often happens for me, and I realized, perhaps for the very first time, that no matter how tragically shortened Steve's life was, I know for a fact that he left this earth a happy man who knew he was very, very loved. Even Sharon, with whom Colton is still very close (Terry recently passed away), has expressed how relieved and glad she is that Steve moved forward from his first marriage, difficult though that was, because he found happiness for a decade with me—the kind of incredible love that some people never experience, but that I have been gifted with twice. Receiving that knowledge, I felt yet another wound inside me close over. I expect these moments will continue to happen for the rest of my life.

This summer, Michael and I plan to renew our vows, and though we haven't been the big international travelers I was in my previous marriages, we're planning to go to Portugal and Amsterdam. "I'm tired of talking about these things," Michael said to me. "We just need to do them. Life is precious."

A thing that can't be explained to the young is how there is something about the urgency of older love—the fear of running out of time—that has less in common with the middle years of raising kids and focusing on careers or homes and more in common with the blush of young love, where every day feels like a marvel, a lifetime unto itself.

If that is not a happy ending . . . well, I don't really know what is.

Still, one more thing before I go . . .

One night not long ago, during Colton's junior year at Pepperdine, he called wanting to review with me details of the "Mattress Story."

This story is famous in our family—even to Colton, who was not yet born when it took place—because it embodies so much of who Steve was that I've been telling it to the boys for as long as they can remember. It was, for them, like hearing about the Three Little Pigs or reading *Goodnight Moon*—like lore of Santa coming down the chimney, only in this case Santa was their father and he was, once upon a time, very very real.

I wasn't physically present for the Mattress Story either, but I've told it so many times I know it better than certain stories of my own life. It goes like this:

One morning, a vibrant, fortyish, and, if I do say so myself, extremely handsome man is driving to work at Cantor Fitzgerald in Manhattan. He is listening to the radio, driving on FDR like any other day, possibly thinking about something he has to do in the office or maybe—let's say—thinking about his wife or his young son, Brett, smiling to himself a bit at the memory of their faces when he left that morning, still warm from sleep and smiling goodbyes at him.

The man has no idea that in all too short a time the Cantor Fitzgerald offices will be blown out of existence by a fiery plane. He has no idea that for most of the years his surviving family will tell this story, he will already be dead. Right now, he doesn't even know there will be a story to tell—he's just listening to some morning talk radio when suddenly something the morning show host says catches his attention: *I just want to throw this out there*, the morning host is saying, barely past 5:00 a.m. on a weekday, nothing but commuters on the other end of his voice, most of the world still asleep. *We got a call this morning from a single mother who said she and her four kids are all sleeping in one room on the floor because they don't have any mattresses. We'd love to get some callers in case anyone wants to pitch in toward a mattress fund for the kids.*

The host gives the number to call, a familiar number to the commuters who numbly listen to this show every morning as they drive into the city. Perhaps he throws in *Every dollar helps*, that familiar adage of radio fundraisers. Does the morning host sound tired, too, at this early hour, or is he irrationally peppy after being up all night, set to crash after his morning gig?

The phone isn't exactly ringing off the hook back at the radio station. Cell phones aren't universal yet; the iPhone won't be invented for many years yet. But Steve's got himself a newfangled smartphone, a BlackBerry—all the top people at Cantor Fitzgerald do—and before he knows he's even doing it, exactly, his fingers are punching in the number to the station. As the phone rings, he wonders if maybe he'll get some kind of voicemail—but no, someone answers, and in no time he's being passed over to the host.

"Hey," Steve says, his voice warm and friendly—the kind of voice that puts people immediately at ease. "I'd like to buy those kids mattresses. All of them, the mother too."

"Wow," the host says, clearly surprised. He wasn't expecting it to be this easy. So few things in life are easy. He wasn't expecting one man to call instantly and offer to take care of it all in one fell swoop. But this—this is morning show gold! The audience is going to love this!

The host signals the producer, keeps Steve on the line while he calls the woman back so she can get on the radio, too, and talk to this guy, this benefactor. And then, before you know it, that's exactly what's happening: Steve and the mother are talking to each other and the woman is crying.

"My kids don't have to sleep on the floor tonight," the woman says, like it is a thing she can't believe—a thing she never expected to be given. The relief in her voice is palpable.

Steve has never known that kind of desperation, that kind of hardship. He's led a life that feels charmed; he's the happiest guy he knows. And so he says, "Look, I want you to buy bunk beds for them too. I want you to buy all the bedding, whatever you need."

The woman he is talking to is stunned. But I, the woman telling you this story, am not. That is just how Steve Cherry was.

We're in trouble and I'm trying to get all the young mothers to safety.

In less than two years, that will be the last sentence anyone alive ever hears him say.

Now, twenty one years after his death, the son who doesn't remember him will say to his professor in the speech class, "I'm going to give a speech about my father, and I don't know what's going to happen. I might get emotional."

The professor will seem worried, unsure whether he should allow him to proceed.

But Steve Cherry's son Colton will nail the speech. He will not panic; he will not freeze; his limbs will not go numb and stop working; he will not lose the ability to swallow and have to be shuttled home early to lie as still as a plank as his mother did at his brother's wedding just a handful of months ago. He has known, his entire life, that his father watches out for him. He doesn't talk about it much. In fact, he rarely talks about his father at all, except to those with whom he is very intimate. No one in this speech class had any idea his father was killed on 9/11 until today.

When class is out, another student will catch up to Colton in the parking lot. They aren't friends. They've never had a conversation. The guy—maybe he's wearing a baseball cap, a Pepperdine sweatshirt—will be a little out of breath, like Colton left class quickly and he had to run to reach him before he got into his car and drove away. The other student will call Colton's name to get his attention, and Colton will turn, his face slightly red from emotion, to face the other young man.

"Hey, dude," the guy will say. "I don't know your dad, but I'll tell you this—he is one proud man tonight of the son you turned out to be."

Shortly after the first love of my life died—back when Russ was just an extended family member I'd met casually a handful of times, back when I had never laid eyes on Michael, back when I had no idea how I was even going to live through each day without the molecules of my body detaching from one another and floating away or the ground opening up to swallow me in my grief, much less how I was supposed to get through the rest of my life—I made one promise to myself. I vowed that I would make Steve proud of his sons. That I would raise them to be fine young men.

All these years later, with the scars on both my body and my heart to mark the passing years, I am here to say that I've done my job. I am beyond proud of the two men they have become. And I know Steve is too.

Brett and Colton embody the best of all three of their fathers—of Steve, of Russ, of Michael. And it's that knowledge that helps me to understand that everything I've been through—the good, the bad, the ugly—is nothing I can regret. It was only through every one of these loves, however spectacular or imperfect, and every one of these losses that my sons

THE ROAD TO YESTERDAY

have become the precious, loving, generous, and kindhearted men they are.

The Road to Yesterday is one I travel all the time, every day, because even as I walk this new road as a wife and a mother, I will always be a widow: These two roads are, in many ways, the same road—separate in time but merged forever in my heart, in every beat and in every moment of my life.

On this road I have come full circle, knowing I kept the most important vow I ever made.

We did it, Steve.

Until we meet again in the stardust.

ACKNOWLEDGMENTS

I will forever be grateful to my incredible ghostwriters Gina Frangello and Emily Rapp Black for making my dream a reality. This journey of putting my story into words was deeply personal, and your dedication, patience, and expertise helped bring it to life in ways I could have never imagined. I could not have asked for better collaborators in this process. Thank you for your creativity, your professionalism, and, most importantly, your belief in this project.

For the gift of their time, I would like to extend my heartfelt gratitude to the fearless group of women who helped me launch this book. To my editing team at The Stable Book Group, Brooke Warner, Krissa Lagos, and Addison Gallegos. To my BookSparks publicity team: Crystal Patriarche, who became a fast friend over our very first lunch, Tabitha Bailey, and Grace Fell. Without all of you, this dream of mine would never have become a reality.

To this day, my heart is filled with love and gratitude for the endless support from my family and friends who showed up for me when I needed you most. To my brother David, I don't think I could have survived all the dark days without you. You are My Rock and I am beyond blessed and lucky to be your favorite sister. Thank you to Gina, Anne and Chris, Laney, Jana, Cheryl, Bo, Diane, Sandy and Connie, Greg,

Laura and Kenny, for stepping in and literally taking care of me. You made living bearable.

To Michael, my silver lining, thank you for believing in me as I took on this project. I could not have done it without your support and endless love. I still look into your bright and beautiful blue eyes, as I did the very first time in Victor, and know how lucky I am that you came into my life and saved me. You complete me, my love.

To Brett and Colton, you have been a mother's dream come true. After losing your father, we became The Three Musketeers. In my darkest days, it was the two of you that kept me going. You are the reason I got out of bed each and every morning. You gave me the strength to keep fighting. I have watched you grow, with such admiration, into two of the finest, most respectful, and loving young men. You make this world a better place and I am beyond proud to call you my sons.

Finally, to Steve, our hero. Thank you for taking your beautiful and soulful voice to Nashville, just a few months before 9/11, to record *The Road to Yesterday*. Hearing your words, I believe you knew that you had to leave me. I know you left this world a happy and fulfilled man. I am blessed to have shared our years together. You were taken from us way too soon, yet I have always known that you are right there looking after me and our beautiful boys, guiding and protecting us. I have always thought that your last words on this earth were "Please God, take care of my girl." He certainly has, and then some...

ABOUT THE AUTHOR

Hillary Mayberry

Maryellen Donovan was born and raised in Stamford, Connecticut. The youngest of four children and the mother of two sons, family is everything to her. Maryellen lives with her husband, Michael, in Hailey, Idaho—a magical valley she considers to be her true home sweet home.

Looking for your next great read?

We can help!

Visit www.shewritespress.com/next-read
or scan the QR code below for a list
of our recommended titles.

She Writes Press is an award-winning
independent publishing company founded to
serve women writers everywhere.